STORIED

STORIED

POEMS, LYRICS & UNSPOKEN THOUGHTS

MEGAN KATARINA

Paperback ISBN: 9798988638605
Case Laminate Hardcover ISBN: 9798988638612
eBook ISBN: 9798988638629

POE000000 POETRY / General
MUS052000 MUSIC / Lyrics
POE023000 POETRY / Subjects & Themes / General

Cover design and typesetting by Kaitlin Barwick
Edited by Valene Wood

www.megankatarina.com

This book is dedicated to:

Mom, my best friend and confidant. I am in awe of what you've overcome in this life and inspired by how big you love in spite of it all. I love your pure heart.

Dad, memorizer of Robert Service and singer of silly songs. Thank you for giving me a love for the outdoors and the truth. You're the reason I am brave.

Rayna, my sissy and friend. I've been looking up to your heart, humor, and authenticity since my first breath.

To my dearest nieces and nephews: Landon, Nina, Raelyn, Emerson, Arlo, and Tatum. Being your aunt is one of my greatest joys and honors in life. I hope that I inspire you to follow your heart always!

Lastly, I dedicate this to all the misfits doodling in the margins, getting teased, and nursing broken hearts. Always be yourself. You are the lights of the world!

CONTENTS

INITIATION

STORIED'S SECRET ALBUM

What makes *Storied* special is that it is not just a poetry book. This book includes a *Secret Album* created for readers only. As you turn the pages in this book, you will happen upon 22 DIFFERENT SONGS sprinkled throughout the book. I have recorded these songs so that you can listen along as you read. Although some of these songs have been previously recorded, I have included new, updated versions of them. There are also many never-before-heard songs included in this album. Listen and enjoy as you read along!

HOW TO ACCESS THE SECRET ALBUM:

To get the password to the album playlist, please visit this link on your computer or cell phone and enter your email:

www.megankatarina.com/storiedalbum

When you encounter pages with this symbol, that is your cue to visit the secret album's page to listen to the track number that is on the symbol.

Lastly, if you'd rather experience this album on a physical CD, you can order it here:

www.megankatarina.com/shop

INTRODUCTION

As I write this introduction, I'm sitting in a chair on my porch overlooking my garden. It's late January of 2023, and a "chilly" 60 degrees, by Florida standards. Today I'm taken back to when this project began. It was born into existence as an idea in 2019 after my national house concert tour. Going from town to town, sharing my poetry and music with the audience at all my shows sparked a desire within me to create that magical experience in book form. Then, in late 2021, I put pen to paper, or rather, fingers to keyboard, and began recording all of my poems.

For some, this might seem a simple process; however, for a songwriter, this task was more daunting than the actual writing of the book. For almost a year I hunted through all my musings, spread between thirty different journals over a span of two decades. I got sidetracked a million times in my rantings about dating or mean teachers, dog-eared and sticky-noted countless pages, until finally, my collection of poetry and writings were all in one place.

I thought this was where the hard work ended. After all, it is a poetry book, and all the poems are already written. But once I began working toward editing, publishing, and organizing, I noticed something big was missing in this book: The Story. And as I began sharing stories and piecing them together, I realized the story wasn't just a missing piece, it was the central piece.

You will find that this book is in chronological order, as most stories are. I have tried to structure this story using my favorite narrative in mythology called the Hero's Journey. The Hero's Journey is a very common story structure in folklore that is defined by its three main components: the Departure, the Initiation, the Return. I bet you can come to your own correct conclusions of what the components mean just by relating those three words to your own life. But for me, this means the naïve longing for romance and adventure, the inevitable loss of innocence and hope that comes with going out on your own, and finally, the balance and wisdom you attain in the end thanks to the lessons learned from those experiences.

Just a disclaimer, I don't consider myself a hero to anyone else, but rather, I consider us all our own hero, or protagonist of our unique story. The beautiful thing about a human life is it's not just one story. It's many stories woven together. And most of them contain my second favorite element in narratology, a moral.

This book is a collection of my experiences, the lessons learned, and the wisdom I gained throughout my twenty-six years of life, sewn like patches of a quilt into a coming-of-age tale. I weave my poetry and experiences together through story because I believe that story is what is missing in modern-day art. And since story is missing in our culture, it is missing in our own lives. This saddens me because this ancient art that our ancestors gave to us is what relates us, teaches us, heals us, and shows us we are not alone in our human experience. And in the end, it is all we have to pass along to those after us.

This is the story of my life thus far, told through my art. My greatest hope is that in reading this you see your own story and remember the power that it has in your life.

ORIGIN

When I was in elementary school, I discovered Shel Silverstein and fell in love immediately. I was fascinated with the simple way he can turn a funny phrase into something that makes you think. You'll find that in these childhood poems, Shel is who I was emanating. The way he rhymes and turns phrases has stuck with me all my years, instilling a love for expressing myself in a profound way using practical language.

So here are a few poems I wrote in grade school. We all start somewhere, and even if it feels incredibly goofy for me to be sharing these (which it does), they are important to share, because it takes many mistakes and funny creations to hone a craft. Read them to your kids, if ya got 'em. Read them to your dogs. Or just simply read them to yourself and celebrate the fact that we all start somewhere.

Singing with Dad.

The front cover of my first songwriting book.

SMALL

Written 2004

I'm very small,
Smaller than my dog's bouncy ball,
To me, what is loud is a whistle call,
And it's extremely dangerous to go to the mall,
Because I'm so small.

Sometimes I sit down and cry little tears,
Because I'm smaller than a baby's ears,
And because I'm so small I have many fears,
And I just wear small pieces of clothes,
because I'm too small for clothes from Sears.

And how I shrunk,
It's all a daze,
It doesn't matter anyways,
The important thing is that I'm puny,
And because I'm small I look quite loony.

Now that I'm done, go tell your friends
Of my little story, that begins and ends.

GOD OF POEMS

Written 2005

One day I went to see the god of poems,
He had 42 little poem gnomes,
Who brushed their hair with little combs,
And when I tried to talk to them, they only said poems.

So I said poem guy,
I've tried to write but I fail every try,
Can't you give me a poem that I can buy?
He put down his cane and said with a sigh,
I'll give you poem powers if you give me a pie.

And so I gave him a pie,
And I got my poem powers,
Goodbye.

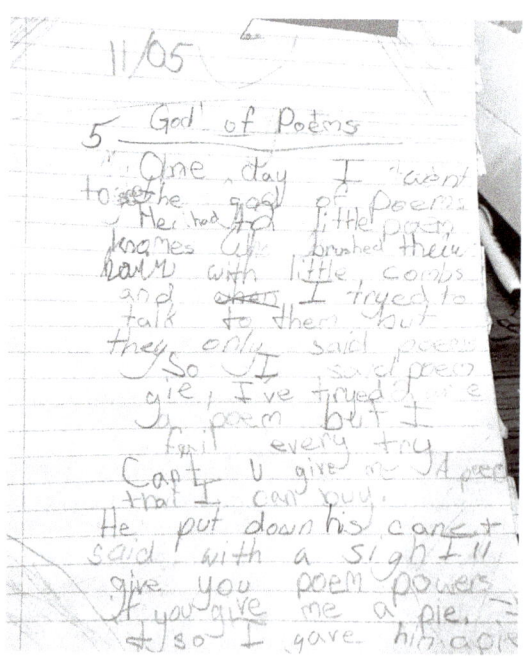

SLEEP CENTER

Written 2005

One day I went to the sleep center,

And for two hours I did sleep,

But those darn meeps

(They are creatures who steal your sleep),

They took my poor sleep,

And donated it to a sheep,

So now at night I can not sleep,

I toss and turn and then I weep,

So if you ever go to a center for sleep,

Do not sleep!

SMILE

Written 2005

No, I will not smile,

Not for you or my friend Kyle,

Not for taking off a day of fixing the tile,

Well, maybe . . .

OK, I'll smile.

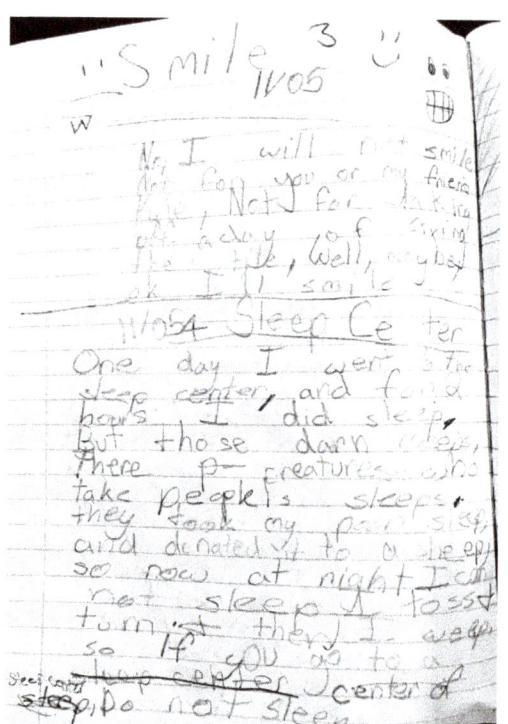

PUPPIES ARE BETTER THAN BOYS

Written 2008

Puppies are better than boys,
They are cute and soft and fun,
They don't make up stupid ploys
And it's ok to have more than one!

Puppies are better than boys,
And when puppies are rowdy it's cute,
They silently play with their toys,
While boys are much better on mute.

Puppies are better than boys,
They aren't mean and they listen to you,
They obviously outshine boys,
So they're better, now tell me something new!

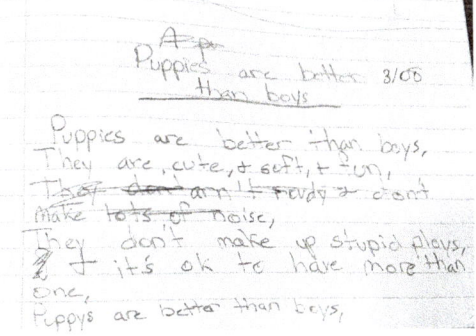

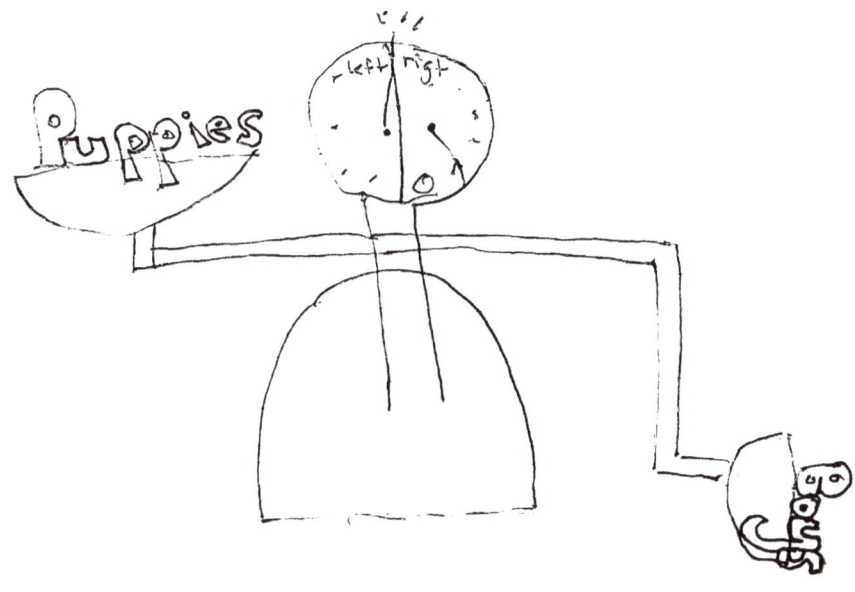

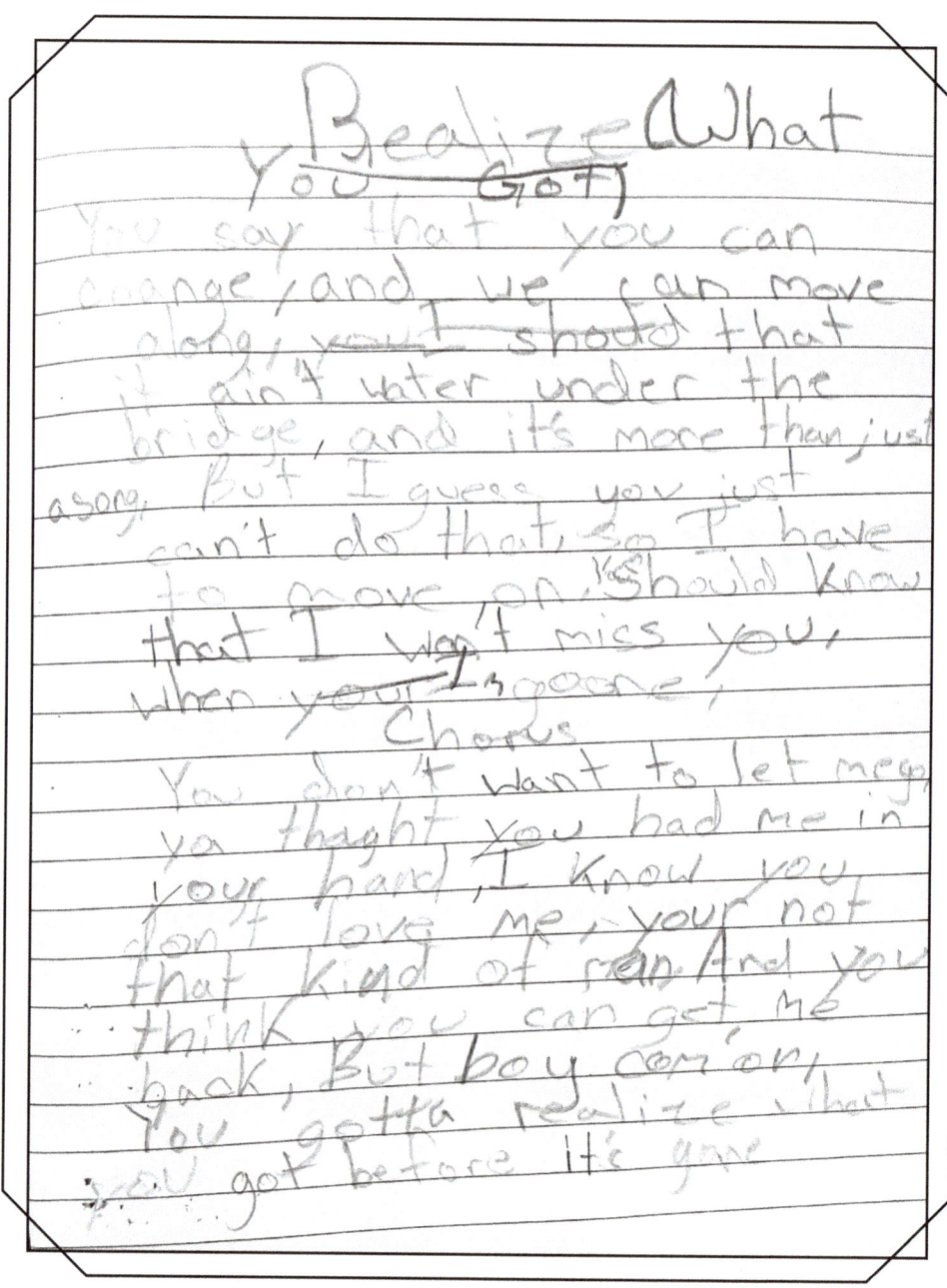

Realize (What You Got)

You say that you can change, and we can move along, you I shoud that it ain't water under the bridge, and it's more than just a song. But I guess you just can't do that, so I have to move on, Should know that I won't miss you, when your gone,

Chorus

You don't want to let me go, ya thught you had me in your hand, I know you don't love me, your not that kind of man. And you think you can get me back, But boy c'mon, you gotta realize what you got before it's gone

This is one of the first songs I remember writing in fifth grade.

ORIGIN

There is nobleness in skill and craft

And strategies for winning,

But none of them as true

As the sweet virtue

Of just simply,

Beginning

Trying to learn guitar with my dad around age six.

DEPARTURE

You can't have a good tale without a departure. Whether physical or metaphorical, we all depart in some way to go on a quest for something missing. Something we believe we can't find within ourselves. Usually the quest is for belonging, for adventure, or for love. In my case, it was all of the above.

I used to watch rom-coms on repeat from the time I was ten years old well into my early twenties. It didn't matter how many times I'd seen the movie, what mattered was the feeling that it gave me to watch two people find love in "adversity." I was the textbook definition of a hopeless romantic.

Something important to note about hopeless romantics is, not only can they not wait to fall in love, they can't wait to experience the drama of it. I have a really distinct memory of my sister, who's ten years older than me, going through her first heartbreak. I snuck under her bed and read her journals. I remember reading something along the lines of, "I will never fall in love again." As a nine-year-old, I could not fathom or begin to imagine what could make someone feel things this deep. My sister is very dear to me, and I did not relish her going through such a painful time. But looking back now as an adult, I can see what an impact witnessing that experience had on me. The weirdest thing is, witnessing that heartbreak didn't make me want to avoid love, it made me want to capture it the first chance I got and feel as much as I could.

It reminds me of this scene in one of my favorite movies since childhood called *Practical Magic* starring Nicole Kidman and Sandra Bullock. They are both young girls secretly observing as their aunts, who are witches, treat a woman who comes in late at night. Distraught and lovesick, the woman begs them to make the man she loves want her fiercely. The girls watch as a bird is sacrificed and the spell is performed for the woman. Then, Sandra Bullock's younger character says, "I'm never going to fall in love," to which Nicole Kidman's younger character replies, "I can't wait to fall in love."

It's me. I'm Nicole Kidman.

But, hopeless romantics are not just romantic about love, they're romantic about life. And after spending so much of my childhood as a loner, longing for love, I got tired of dreaming and I decided if I couldn't have love, I would go fall in love with the world. As soon as I turned eighteen, I set off in my truck and camped wherever I could find a spot. When I lived in Florida, I'd drive to the Keys for the weekend or Fort Myers Beach. I slummed it and bummed boat rides off of friends I would make meandering around town. I snorkeled and paddled and fell in love with the underwater wildlife. When I moved to Nashville, I couldn't convince any of my friends to go with me, so I would spend a lot of my weekends alone, a few hours out of the city, hiking and camping. I'm pretty sure I've hiked to every waterfall within a two-hundred-mile radius of Nashville. I just couldn't sit still.

At age twenty-three, following the release of my album, *Being Crazy Ain't for the Weak*, I spent almost six months of 2019 touring across the country to play house concerts. I stayed in the houses of my hosts, and when I was between shows, I camped in a tent at national parks. I traveled on my own from Tennessee, through the Midwest, to Portland, down through California, and then to Maine and back! I played show after show in new places and watched in humble amazement as my songs and stories turned the strangers I was playing for into family. It was beautiful, scary, sometimes dangerous, hilarious, dirty, difficult, and ultimately rewarding. Yet, I still found I was crying myself to sleep most nights. A guttural sense of loneliness that started in my heart slowly took over my whole body. And although traveling made me happy, it didn't change the fact that I was running.

My longing for love and my love for travel are closely tied for this reason. They are true aspects of who I am, but they are also tangled in my tendency towards escapism. I used them to distract myself from my struggles with mental illness. And my struggles with mental illness made my life a steady stream of extreme highs and lows. Broken heart? Time to plan another trip! Exhausted from traveling? Time to fall in love and obsess over the relationship! I gained wisdom and experience from these decisions, but I put off the learning of the lesson because I never took time to process what I learned from it all. It was too overwhelming for me at the time. I just kept running.

So for many years, I lived my life on a swinging pendulum between love and adventure, misery and ecstasy, confusion and clarity. This was the lens through which I experienced my life. I wouldn't change a thing, because all of those experiences gave me the poems and prose I have for you in this chapter. Spanning between the years of 2010 and 2018, or ages thirteen to twenty-two, this is the story of my own Departure and the love and adventures that came with it.

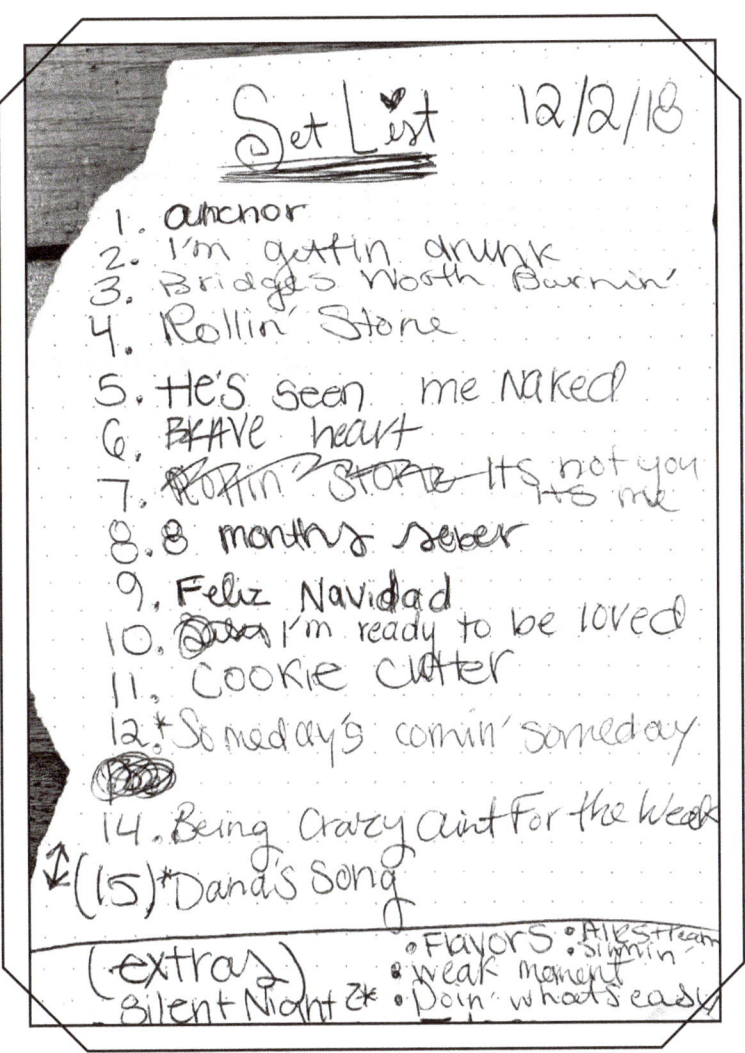

The first set list I ever wrote up for a house concert!

SOMETIMES

Written 2010; Recorded by Megan Katarina on album *Megan Katarina*, track 2

None of the songs on the radio are about you
But they're all about you
And none of the faces in a photograph are your face
But I see your face
And sometimes, I'm always thinking 'bout you

When it's pouring down outside
I wonder if you're doing alright
And when the wind's wrestling the trees
I wonder if you're thinking about me
'Cause sometimes I'm always thinking 'bout you

When I'm at home and I'm singing out loud
I'm not singing for you
But I'm singing for you
When I make a mistake, I may tell the crowd
it's my fault
But it's always your fault
And sometimes, I'm always thinking 'bout you

When it's pouring down outside
I wonder if you're doing alright
And when the wind's wrestling the trees
I wonder if you're thinking about me
'Cause sometimes I'm always thinking 'bout you

I wouldn't call it an obsession
Just a thought that won't move along
This is just a blue reflection
This is not a love song

Now it's pouring down outside
I wonder how you're doing tonight
And the winds wrestling the trees
Baby tell me are you thinking about me
Yeah the waves have flooded the shore

I'm not lying anymore, if you need the truth
I'm always thinking 'bout you

SOMETIMES

Since I was able to hold a pencil, I was writing songs. But something happened around the time I turned thirteen, when I taught myself to play guitar. My writing began its transformation from a little girl just trying to mimic what she heard on the radio, to a young woman writing what she felt.

This was the age I began to get very serious about my songwriting. After a year of talking about nothing but Nashville, my parents finally relented and began taking me on trips up there to play shows and network with other writers. I was obsessed. I went to workshops, read books, and dedicated myself fully to the craft. The calluses on my hands opened and bled constantly because of my addiction to having my hands on a guitar.

At the time, I was doing this exercise called freewriting, where, as soon as you open your eyes in the morning, you immediately begin writing every thought that comes to mind. No filter, no judgment, and no stopping to edit. The whole point of the exercise was just to write. I did this for ten minutes every day.

So, one day I woke up and began freewriting. Among all the nonsense that poured out of my head and onto the page were the words, "Sometimes, I'm always thinking about you." I read back and circled it, meaning it was an idea I could work with. Then I finished this song later that day.

MIRROR, MIRROR

Written 2012; Recorded by Megan Katarina on album *Trouble*, track 9

I could pack my things and leave right now
Drive fifty miles or so out of town
Or maybe go until I'm out of gas
Just trying to find some happiness to last

I could stay right here and do the same things
Tempted into sins and the joy they bring me
I could run away with a boy who don't need me
But where would any of these choices leave me

Mirror mirror on the wall
Please tell me
I'm staring into you but I'm all I can see
Except I don't know this girl at all
This question I can't understand
Please, mirror mirror
Tell me who I am

I could get a diary and write it all down
Look inside myself till maybe I'm found
I could go to church and ask to help me find sight
Of the difference of what's wrong and what's right

Mirror mirror on the wall
Please tell me
I'm staring into you but I'm all I can see
Except I don't know this girl at all
This question I can't understand
Please, mirror mirror
Tell me who I am

On the pursuit of happiness what's the limit
What's this life and how do I know what to do with it

Mirror mirror on the wall
Please tell me
I'm staring into you but I'm all I can see
Except I don't know this girl at all
This question I can't understand
Please, mirror mirror
Tell me who I am

MIRROR, MIRROR

In my sophomore year of high school, a popular kid convinced me to ride to a hotel in Daytona with her and some guy we didn't know so she could say she was sleeping over at my house. I was her scapegoat. I agreed, and we snuck off to Daytona.

Unfortunately, because this was definitely not her first time doing this, her parents caught on, told my parents, and we got busted. My parents were so appalled that I would lie to them like that, because I was generally a pretty well-behaved kid. My dad got so angry it was absolutely devastating to me. Hungover, ashamed, and lacking sleep, he made me scrub the baseboards all day. When I was allowed to take a break, I wrote this song.

It breaks my heart to read these lyrics and look back on that sixteen-year-old girl trying to figure out who she was and her place in this world. I'm so glad I finally leaned into song-writing and my faith in God. This is what saved me ultimately, and brought me down the path of becoming my true self.

VINTAGE SOUL, GYPSY HEART

Written 2015

Night sky in the middle of a desert
Shot of whiskey to drown out the pain
Neon light in a honky-tonk corner
White dress with a motor oil stain

I saw you across the room
And you started walking up
You asked me what's my story
So I just said what I thought

Vintage soul, and a gypsy heart
Hung a map and threw a dart
Made a wish upon a star
Opened my eyes and there you are
Outlaw mind on a long highway
Partly smart, partly insane
I swore that I would never stay
But you could come along
With Me

Thrift dress in an old cantina
Bare feet in the late July rain
Know my faults but tell me I'm flawless
Confess my sins but I don't feel any shame

Tomorrow I'll be packing up
Cause that's just what I do
Never really had a knack for love
But it never felt this true

Vintage soul, and a gypsy heart
Hung a map and threw a dart
Made a wish upon a star
Opened my eyes and there you are
Outlaw mind on a long highway
Partly smart, partly insane
I swore that I would never stay
But you could come along
With Me

I've felt pain like the poison of a rattlesnake
Loneliness as cold as ice
All this time I was running from something wrong
Maybe I've been running towards something
Right

Vintage soul, and a gypsy heart
Hung a map and threw a dart
Made a wish upon a star
Opened my eyes and there you are
Outlaw mind on a long highway
Partly smart, partly insane
I swore that I would never stay
But you could come along
With Me

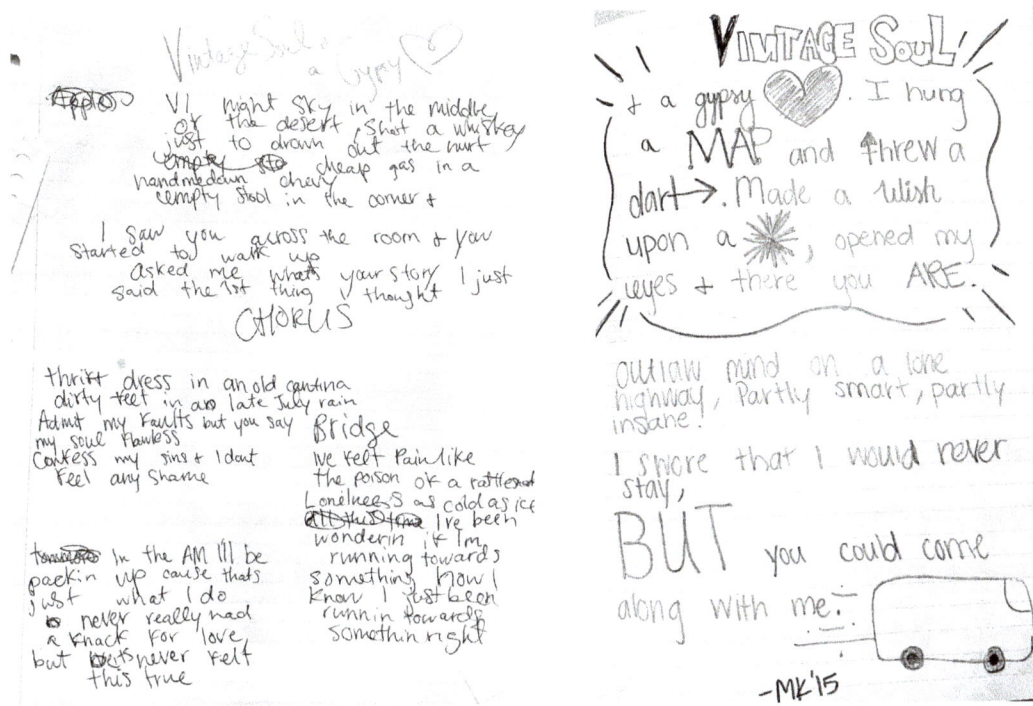

VINTAGE SOUL, GYPSY HEART

I got the idea for this song when I was up really late on a trip to North Carolina with my parents. We were doing a lot of hiking and exploring, and I was thinking about the fact that I wanted my life to feel like this—an adventure. More than that, I wanted whoever I fell in love with to be an extension of that. This was my manifestation love song to whoever would hold my hand on the adventures of the future!

COOKIE CUTTER

Written July 2015; Recorded by Megan Katarina on Digital EP 3, track 2

I don't sell music with my butt or even with my face
I sell music with the truth of words I have to say
I don't follow hip trends just to hear song get played
It ain't my thing

If you got stripes and they got spots, they're gonna push you down
Tell you that it's bad to be the odd one in the crowd
If you're like me, a zebra in a pasture full of cows
You ain't wrong
Just cause you don't belong

I ain't low enough to make it in your high society
I'd rather climb my way up to the top than play dirty and cheat
Rather get blisters on my hand standing up for what I believe
Than be another, like every other
Cookie Cutter

That goes out to anyone who walks a jagged line
Tell that straight-edged ruler being different ain't a crime
In a world that's selling bullshit wouldn't you just rather buy
Something real
Than take an easy deal

I ain't low enough to make it in your high society
I'd rather climb my way up to the top than play dirty and cheap
Rather get blisters on my hand standing up for what I believe
Than be another, like every other
Cookie Cutter

Oh hearts and stars can be great
But I'd rather be my own shape

I ain't low enough to make it in your high society
I'd rather climb my way up to the top than play dirty and cheap
Rather get blisters on my hand standin' up for what I believe
Than be another, like every other
Cookie Cutter

COOKIE CUTTER

My relationship with country music is complicated. For many years, I was proud of the genre I was raised on and I wanted to be part of a movement to bring it back to its traditional roots. I'm talking about the greats. A few names that come to mind are Dolly Parton, Merle Haggard, Johnny Cash, John Prine, Loretta Lynn, Kris Kristofferson, Emmylou Harris, and so many more. I meet a lot of people who don't love country music but enjoy Johnny Cash. Why is this? Because he tells great stories, of course! This music was so beautiful to me for the way it created beautiful imagery in my mind of the lives of others. It was so brutally honest too. It captivated me and inspired me to tell my own stories.

Sadly, over the past twenty years, the genre has drifted further and further from its hallowed past and turned into mostly shallow ramblings about "country life." By being immersed in this new country music culture, I saw firsthand the irreverence and disregard for the roots of country music and the way commercialism and greedy executives had molded this new version of the genre. There's a popular saying that country music is "three chords and the truth." But lately there's a missing key ingredient—truth.

I wrote this song almost a decade ago. In my bed, past midnight, while thinking about the uphill battle I had ahead of me with my music. For many years, I had a lot of anger about the lack of opportunity for women, and just storytellers in general. But over the years now, I have found my place amongst the fans who appreciate lyricism and story. I've weaved in and out of country music, going wherever it is that I can be myself. And though I may never achieve great fame, at least I've always stayed true to my vow, not to sell out and be another, like every other, cookie cutter.

ANCHOR

Written July 2016; Recorded by Megan Katarina on album *Being Crazy Ain't For The Weak*, track 2

Sweet habits of self-destruction
Start out as an innocent thing
I just wanted to feel love in
All the glory and trouble it brings
I should've gave up long ago
Hit the surface and shed my shame
Didn't realize I'd become
Addicted to feeling the pain

Till a year later leaning on the refrigerator on the floor
Jonesin' for more

When you're in love with an anchor
You learn to hold your breath
A quick drop to the bottom from the top and
You'll justify the rest
But I'm only bound by
Rope I wrapped around
On my own
So down I go

I guess I should feel more tragic
Wrapped up in my misery
But I live in a state of numbness
I have accepted defeat
And I don't blame the anchor
He does what he's built to do
But if I hold on to the parts worth saving
I'm holding the ugly too

I tried using all my might to force us to the top
I guess I forgot

When you're in love with an anchor
You learn to hold your breath
A quick drop to the bottom from the top and
You'll justify the rest
But I'm only bound by
Rope I wrapped around
On my own
So down I go

And the anchor's in love with me
But the anchor can't stay afloat
If I could wish away gravity
I wouldn't have to let go

But I'm in love with an anchor
I'm dying for a breath
I'll leave the bottom for the top
And I'll fill my lungs with air
While wishing I was bound by
Rope that I left down below
But Up I go

Up I go

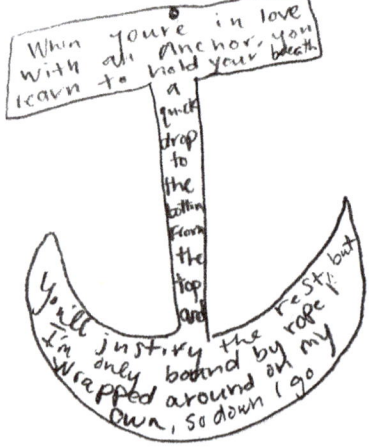

Anchor ©July 30, 2016
Megan Klaut

Sweet habits of self destruction
start out as an innocent
thing I just wanted to feel
love in all the glory & trouble it
brings, I didn't mean...
I shoulda let go long ago
but the surface free of my shame... I thought saved us
...feelin the pain
til a year later leanin' on the bridge...
on the floor, jonesin for more

- CHORUS -
When your in love w/an anchor
you learn to hold your breath
a quick drop to the bottom
from top
you'll justify the rest
but I'm wrapped around by
rope that... on my own
so down I go

I guess I should tell more
tragic & wrapped up in my
misery but I live in a state of numbness
I have accepted defeat
& I don't blame the anchor
he does what he's built to do
but if I hold onto the
parts worth saving I'm holding

the... too
I tried to... in a...
swimmin to the top
but the weights too strong

CHORUS   usin' I tried
to force to the top
guess I forgot
                  that

bridge
the strength & the weight
the pull & the gravity

Its only bad because I'm... only do what we should
& the anchors in love w/me too
but the anchor can't stay afloat
I'm... If I... wish...away
in a world w/o gravity
I wouldn't have to let go

CHORUS
But   dying for a breath
I cant just hold
I'll drop I'll leave the bottom for the top
& I'll kill my lungs w/ air
while & wishing I was
bound by rope that I left down
below but up I go

ANCHOR

I consider this song the most important song in my catalogue because of the connection it has brought me with my fans. When I was nineteen, I started dating someone who was much older than me. He was always gone playing shows and the relationship was not a quality one. I had to let him go because he was dragging me down. I was up until 2 a.m. thinking about all this one night and I wrote this terribly depressing poem about being dragged down by an anchor and dying. The next thing I knew, the melody of the chorus came to me. I didn't want to write it, it was too heartbreaking, but I had to. The whole song just came through me right then. Looking back, my situation wasn't that drastic, but I've had fans message me about leaving abusive relationships because of this song. That is the reason I write.

THEM/ME

Written November 2016

THEM.

She's making it up
She just wants attention
Her mind's not a monster
It's just her invention
Those aren't real tears
She's an actor on cue
She's only crying
To see what you'll do
If she really felt
What she swears she feels
We'd be able to see it
It must not be real
Why is her smile
So bright and inviting
If she's being wrecked
By the demons she's fighting
Beautiful and blessed
She can't be insane
Too free and creative
To be bound by chains
We all have our days
It can't be that bad
Depression? Anxiety?
No, she's just sad

ME.

I'm crazy, I know it
I smile and joke
The doctors, the drugs
It's all just a hoax
I nod and agree
It's not worth explaining
I try to suppress it
Quiet, self-shaming
Why should they believe
In an illness they can't see?
How can I blame them?
Sometimes I agree
I look in the mirror
And clutch my own heart
Surprised that my body's
Not falling apart
But my mind must know something
My body doesn't know
Does everyone feel this?
Am I alone?
I make conversation
I laugh at what's funny
They think that I'm charming
Ambitious and sunny
And honestly I adore
Being that girl
Who's so full of life
And in love with the world
But still in good spirits

Darkness is residing
Waiting for a weak moment
To come out of hiding
The slightest of comments
Events or actions
Will set off a land mine
Of fury and passion
The same fire within me
That people admired
Becomes what they resent
And what makes them tired
I try to say sorry
I told you, I'm crazy
They awkwardly laugh
They decide they can't save me

She's just dramatic
They say, but they're wrong
I'm full of weakness
That's why I am strong
Cause you have to have strength
When peace can't be found
An internal prison
Invisible battleground
Happiness finds me and leaves me again
I fight for the good
But sometimes the bad wins.

THEM/ME

I was nineteen years old lying in my bed writhing restlessly when my mom finally convinced me to see a doctor about the anxiety I was having. After filling out a simple Yes or No questionnaire on a clipboard, the doctor glanced at it and said, "Yup, well you have anxiety and depression. I'll prescribe you Zoloft and you can set up the pharmacy with the receptionist." And then she was gone. I took the pills dutifully until I experienced side effects, feeling angry all the time. So, my mom convinced me to go to the doctor again. This time, the doc believed that an antipsychotic drug called Seroquel on top of the Zoloft would do the trick. I took the drugs and began sleeping fifteen hours a day, feeling generally unhinged. Those pills didn't work for me, and the diagnosis itself put so much weight on me that it made me feel even more anxious and depressed. Even though this was only seven or eight years ago, the world has changed a lot regarding mental health stigma, and, at the time, a lot of my friends and family truly thought I was just making it up for attention, which made it that much lonelier.

I went out one Thursday during that time to Cocoa Beach with my best friend to just have some fun and forget about it. We drank, danced, and sang karaoke until the bars closed and it was time to go home. My best friend swore she was fine to drive. And I, being three years younger, believed her. I'll never forget the panic that rose in my chest when the blue lights came on behind us. Some cops had followed us from the bar and, when she blew well over the limit, they were more than happy to throw on those cuffs and bring her to jail. We were lucky to learn that lesson young without hurting ourselves or others that night, but at the time it was terrifying.

There was a deputy that had to wait with me on the side of the road while my parents came to pick me up. He was really kind and we struck up a conversation about his life and about my struggles with my anxiety and how it affects my relationships. I read this poem for him and he was moved. I still remember his name. It was one of those beautiful moments where absolutely nothing makes sense, but you find beauty in life's most unexpected places.

Them

"She's making it up"
"She JUST wants attention"
"Her mind's not a monster,
it's just her invention."
Those aren't real tears,
she's an actor on cue
She's only crying
to see what you'll do
If she ~~really felt~~ really felt
~~the~~ what she swears she feels
We'd be able to see it
It must not be real
Why is her smile
so bright & inviting
If she's being wrecked
by the demons she's fighting
Too free & creative
she can't be insane
→ ~~She makes us laugh~~ Beautiful, & blessed
to be bound by chains
We all have our days
It can't be that bad
Depression? Anxiety? No, she's just sad!

Me

I'm crazy, I know it
I smile & joke
The doctors, the drugs
Its all just a hoax
nod & agree
Its not worth ~~it to~~ ~~agree~~ explaining
I try to suppress it
Quiet & self-shaming
Why should they believe
In illness they can't see?
How can I blame them?
Sometimes I agree.
I look in the mirror
& clutch my own heart
~~I just don't look like a person~~
~~whos falling apart~~
~~my no sign of my body's~~
But my ~~brain~~ mind must
know something, my body doesn't know
Does everyone feel this?
Or am I alone?
↱ I laugh at what's funny
make conversation
they think I am charming
ambitious & sunny/funny
And honestly I ~~too~~ adore
being that girl
whos so full of life
& in love with the world

but still in good ~~moments~~ spirits
the darkness is residing
waiting for a weak moment
to come out of hiding
the slightest of comments,
events, or actions
will set off a landmine
of fury & passion
the same fire w/in me that
people admired
becomes what they resent
and what makes them tired
I try to say sorry
I told you, I'm crazy
They awkwardly laugh
They decide they can't
save me
She's just dramatic, they say
But their wrong
I'm full of weakness, that's
why I look strong
Cause you have to have strength
when peace cant be found
in an internal prison, & invisible
battleground
Happiness finds me then leaves
me again
I fight for the good
but sometimes the bad win

dramatic
energizing
good &
mad

The original flyer for my album release party for "Being Crazy Ain't for The Weak."
In spring of 2018, it broke onto the scene and went #14 on the iTunes country charts.

BEING CRAZY AIN'T FOR THE WEAK

Written December 2016; Recorded by Megan Katarina on album *Being Crazy Ain't For The Weak*, track 12

I warned you when we met
How quickly you forget
I said there's demons here
You said you had no fear

I took a while to fall
And then I surrendered all
You let go of my hand
You don't love what you don't understand

I've got crazy hair
And lazy tears in my clothes
I dream crazy dreams
And rip the seams
That I sew
You like my crazy slippers and crazy kisses
But you don't listen
You amaze me, you won't see
Being crazy ain't for the weak

I was so lost and trapped
And love ain't no map
You were so full of light
And I wanted to ignite

You think the magic's gone
But baby you're the one who's wrong
I've always been this way
You're the one who is afraid

I've got crazy hair
And lazy tears in my clothes
I dream crazy dreams
And rip the seams
That I sew
You like my crazy slippers and crazy kisses
But you don't listen
You amaze me you won't see
Being crazy ain't for the weak

I might break down, I may give in
But I'm more than you have been
I might be broke inside
But look at me I'm still alive

I've got crazy hair
And lazy tears in my clothes
I dream crazy dreams
And rip the seams
That I sew
You like my crazy slippers and crazy kisses
But you don't listen
You amaze me you won't see
Being crazy ain't for the weak

Being Crazy aint For the Weak

I warned you when met, how
quickly you forget,
I said there's demons here,
you said you no fear, I took
a while to fall, & then I surrend-
ered all, I was solost & trapped
love makes a faulty map

— CHORUS —
Ive got crazy hair & lazy
tears in my clothes
I dream crazy dreams
& rip the seams that I sew
You like my crazy slippers & crazy kisses, but
& you amaze me You wont see
that bein crazy aint for the weak
now youre gone my heart bleeds
you wont love what you don't understand
I was so lost & trapped &
love dont work as a map
You were so full of light &
I wanted to ignite
You think the magics gone
but baby your the one whos
wrong we always been this way
your the one who's afraid

Bridge
I may break down
I may give in
But Ive been more than
you have been
I might be broke inside
but look at me
IM STILL ALIVE

BEING CRAZY AIN'T FOR THE WEAK

At the time that I was learning to deal with my diagnosis of anxiety and depression, I was dating someone I considered the love of my life. He didn't understand what I was going through and eventually broke up with me because of it. Everyone has that one person that changes their heart forever, and this guy was mine. So much so, that I wrote an entire album about him!

This breakup happened the day before my family vacation to North Carolina and my parents forced me to still come on the trip. I was upstairs by myself in this cabin crying my eyes out and the line came into my head, "Being crazy ain't for the weak . . ." I wanted him and everyone who misunderstood mental illness to know that it's the opposite of a weakness because it takes so much strength to live with. I wrote this song upstairs and I played it for my family. Since I was very mentally fragile at this time, it made them worried and uncomfortable to hear the song. I felt embarrassed, and sort of put the song away for about six months.

Then, I moved to Nashville the next year and played it for my dear friend and roommate at the time. He loved it, and encouraged me to play it out around town. So, that's what I did. After a year of playing the song at shows, and writing additional songs about my mental health struggles, "Being Crazy Ain't For The Weak" became the title track of the album. It just made sense.

Honestly, I'm incredibly uncomfortable writing this and telling you such vulnerable things about my struggles with mental illness. I know I'm putting myself in a position to be judged. But the thing that keeps me sharing is that I know there is someone reading this who feels like their world is ending. It's not, but only time will make you see that. While that time passes, we can use the stories of those before us as our medicine.

FLAVORS

Written December 2016; Recorded by Megan Katarina on album *To Be Honest*, track 2

I wanna live inside of a houseboat
Lights strung around my makeshift porch
I wanna dwell in a dirty motel
With a broken number on my front door
I wanna light an L with a hippie
Act like a mystery and change my name
I wanna go get drunk with the rich
Just so I can bitch all about the game

I wanna be as many of me as I can be
Cause life's too sweet
To live only one life to savor
I'll cash in my favors
I wanna taste all of the flavors

I wanna half learn ten whole languages
Curse in anguish at my accent
I wanna be an East Mountain momma
Purchase a llama to be my friend
I wanna confuse all humankind
And quote John Prine while I clean my rugs
I wanna learn the millennial knowledge
Flunk out of college and sell free hugs

I wanna be as many of me as I can be
Cause life's too sweet
To live only one life to savor
I'll cash in my favors
I wanna taste all of the flavors

I want more than one bite
Want more than one life
Don't wanna exist
Wanna feel alive

I wanna be as many of me as I can be
Cause life's too sweet
To live only one life to savor
I'll cash in my favors
I wanna taste all of the flavors

Flavors ©M.Klauck
12/17/16

✓ I wanna live inside of
a houseboat lights strung
around my makeshift porch
I wanna dwell in a dirty motel
with a ~~tumbleweed~~
broken ~~it~~ on my kraft
door

✓ I wanna light an L w/a
3 hippie act like a mystery
change my name
I want to get drunk w/
the rich just so I can bitch
all about the game

I wanna 1/2 learn 10
whole languages
curse in anguish at my
~~~~ ~~and~~ east accent
I want to be a ~~best~~ Mountain
Purchase a llama mama
to be mr friend

V 2 I want confuse all human
3 quote J. Prine king
while I clean my rug
I want to learn millenial
knowledge, flunk outta
college 3 sell free
hugs

— CHORUS —

I want to be as many of me
as I can be cause likes
to sweet
to live only one like to savor
I'll cash in my favors
Cause I wanna taste
All of the flavors

bridge Don't wanna end
Wanna feel alive
I want more than 1 bite
~~Live a thousand lives~~
want more than 1 life

FLAVORS

If you've been to one of my live shows, it's likely you've heard the story behind this one. One night in December, my mom and I went to this little sailboat Christmas parade and as we watched the adorable little sailboats float by all lit up, I began to feel dreamy and introspective thinking about life in a houseboat. I walked to the nearest coffee shop for a hot chocolate, and in the bathroom I wrote down this line: "I wanna live inside of a houseboat . . ."

My thinking behind this idea was, how incredible is it that we can live so many different ways, be so many different things, in a lifetime, and yet we can't do it all. You can only live one life, or at most, a few lives, I've learned. That's why I penned this song. Around the time, I was discovering the music of one of my songwriting heroes, John Prine. I must admit, it was his writing style that inspired the quirky, and sometimes nonsensical, lines of this song.

IF THIS AIN'T THE LAST TIME

Written December 2016

He is somethin' like I've never seen
He does what's right and says what he means
He promised forever in exchange for a kiss
And I thought, Lord help me, if he becomes what I miss
So I prayed to God, to ask Him for help
Before I started to feel what I've never felt

If this ain't the last time I fall in love
Please let me know tonight
Because how can I have a heart I can trust
When someone who's wrong feels right
If it's more wasted magic
Then I don't want to have it
Another almost love that lives in my mind
If this ain't the last time

He hasn't called me in three weeks
He says there's reasons for the things happening
But I've tried my best and I can't understand
I've already given my soul to this man
And I thought I knew, and he felt it too
And I cannot help but want this with no one else
'Cause I said

If this ain't the last time I fall in love
Please let me know tonight
Because how can I have a heart I can trust
When someone who's wrong feels right
If it's more wasted magic
Then I don't want to have it
Another almost love that lives in my mind
If this ain't the last time
And when I find the one, how can I give my all
If a piece of me breaks, every time that I fall?

If this ain't the last time that I fall
Then I think I'd rather feel nothing at all
What's the point of the passion?
Of the love without ration?
If someone else is meant to call him mine?
I don't want the memories
If this ain't the last time

IF THIS AIN'T THE LAST TIME

This song is one that didn't make it on the album *Being Crazy Ain't For The Weak,* but I wish it did. I've always felt so passionately about true love, and the commitment that comes with it. I found myself asking the question many of us ask, "Is it really love if it doesn't last forever?"

Maybe this is a juvenile point of view, but what is the point of making those memories with someone, of sharing yourself with someone, all the good and bad, for it to mean nothing in the end? I know people say it does mean something, and that life is about the connections you make along the way. I know I'd be happier if I could learn to let love flow and let go when it's time. But it's still hard for me, even now. I don't necessarily believe in soulmates, but I feel a piece of myself shatter every time I have to let go of someone I thought I would love for life. That's what I wrote this song about. The heartbreaking realization that much of our love will be wasted, forgotten, or at the very best, just a fond memory.

how can I trust my intuition if this wrong one felt so right

- You still remember that love 3 miss it
- You never truly wholly belong to one person when you loved with your entire being 3 soul others
- The promises 3 dreams become lies

(memory)

If this is not the last time I fall then I think I'd rather feel nothing at all

Passion
Romance
Soulmate

how can I have ♡ I can trust if someone wrong felt so right who's

just another almost love that lives Mind
If this aint the last time

v2 He hasnt called me in 3 wks
He says theres reasons
for the things happening

But I've tried my best 3
I cant understand
why should I give me soul
to more than one man?
cause I've already given
my soul to this man I knew
3 he felt it too
I can not help but
want this who one else
cause I said
How can I give the one My whole self
If there is still pieces of My in someone else
bridge
3 when I find the one
how can I give my all
if a break off a piece of me everytime that I fall
breaks everytime that I fall

If this aint the last time I fall in love

© Megan Klauck dec 2016

v1 he is somethin, like I've never seen,
he does whats right, 3 says what he means
People
he promised forever in exchange for a kiss
3 I thought God help me
If he becomes someone I miss
So I prayed to ask him for help
Before I started to feel things I've never felt

— CHORUS —

If this aint the last time I fall in love
Please let me know tonight
I had my share of almost thoughts 3 changin my mind up
I dont wanna make my mind
If its more wasted magic
then I dont wanna have it
cause its passion just waiting to die
Just to learn something felt so right

Final chorus

If this aint the last time that I fall
then I think I'd rather feel nothing at all
cause whats the point of the passion
of the love w/ration
If it just turns into almost enough

I cant always call
one day I will not someone else
If someone else is meant to call him mine
I dont want the memories
If this aint the last ti

HOME IS WHERE YOU PARK IT

Written February 2017

From Washington to Tennessee
To Tupelo to Joshua Tree
And all the places that I haven't been, yet
A Waffle House, a Flying J
A Pilot and a Chick-fil-A
Till I decide which city to stop in

All the play-it-safers like to make a fuss
About the life I'm leading in the name of
Wanderlust
And maybe it's true what they say
That home is where the heart is
But my heart's in a trailer park
And home is where you park it

Well-spinning wheels is not my style
Unless those wheels are putting miles
Behind me in my trusty rusty Ford
Sometimes I'm broke, sometimes I'm rich
Sometimes I laugh, sometimes I bitch
But I can guarantee I'm never bored

All the play-it-safers like to make a fuss
About the life I'm leading in the name of
Wanderlust
And maybe it's true what they say
That home is where the heart is
But my heart's in a trailer park
And home is where you park it

Some people like to stay in place
But I prefer a faster pace
The highway is what makes me feel alive
Some would like to stay at home
But I feel at home when I roam
My driveway is the white and yellow lines

All the play-it-safers like to make a fuss
About the life I'm leading in the name of
Wanderlust
And maybe it's true what they say
That home is where the heart is
But my heart's in a trailer park
And home is where you park it

HOME IS WHERE YOU PARK IT

When I was nineteen, I bought a 1968 Airstream trailer and fixed it up with my dad. I had it for years, but in the end, the consensus was that it was too much of a project to practically keep. So, this year I sold it and bought a Ford Econoline Van, which I also fixed up with my sweet father!

Anyways, around this time of being nineteen and owning a vintage Airstream, I had stars in my eyes thinking about all the places I wanted to travel to. So, this is my silly love song to the nomad life.

Side Note: I got this idea and wrote it in the shower. All the best ideas happen while showering! Or hungover! Or both!

Why I travel:

To find out who I am, apart from who I say I am & who "they" say I am. Who am I when I am not a singer? Who am I in uncertainty? I travel to be humbled, to be @ in service to presence & experience. To learn what I don't know that I don't know. To be thrilled, afraid, delighted, challenged, and opened. To open my mind & heart. I travel for perspective. Because the happiest people are the ones who realize how small they are, are the most at peace. They seek out the specialness of others & see it reflected back in themselves. I travel to make friends with mystery, to marvel at God, to be shown who I really am.

A picture from my visit to Sequoia National Park. I have traveled to California many times to play shows, and I try to enjoy its beauty on my days off as much as possible!

THE WOODS SPARKLE TONIGHT

Written July 2017

The woods sparkle tonight
With lightning bugs, they say
But if I had to I would
Name it magic, anyway

I ponder love I've lost
And love yet to be assumed
Imagining adventures
That have yet to be presumed

And life is but a wave
In which joy will ebb and flow
But here inside this sanction
You would never even know

Gratitude possesses me
And fills me with its light
As the flames dance
And the stars glow

And the woods sparkle tonight
The woods sparkle tonight
Bouncing sweetly tree to tree
But the river isn't bothered
And it carries on dutifully

I'm reminded of my youth
That so-called simpler time
But the hands that made life less than simple
Now, are only mine

I call upon my wisdom
As it seems to reside here
In nature's own sweet stillness
And her chaos without fear

And time will not stop for anyone
In her reckless raging might
But the embers still burn
And the earth still turns
And the woods sparkle tonight

THE WOODS SPARKLE TONIGHT

My childhood was spent outdoors. Every summer and fall, we would take our beat-up old RV to the Smoky Mountains in Tennessee and spend our days tubing in the river, reading books while the rain fell, singing silly campfire songs, hiking, and falling asleep to the lullaby of the rushing river. This place, our secret camping spot on a mountain in Tennessee, shaped who I am and what inspires me.

One night, when I was a teenager, I sat by the campfire with my laptop, writing. The fireflies became active, and the entire woods looked like they were sparkling. I was so in awe of this sight that this poem poured out of me as I reflected on my life so far. This place had become a touchstone for me as I grew up and changed. It just all hit me at once how I keep changing, but those sacred woods are steady and always there for me.

1. WELL ENOUGH ALONE (NOV. 2016)
2. FLAVORS (DEC. 2016)
3. BIG PINE KEY (FEB. 2017)
4. BRIDGES WORTH BURNING (SEPT. 2018)
5. I'M READY TO BE LOVED (NOV. 2018)
6. SOMEDAY'S COMIN' SOMEDAY (NOV. 2018)
7. MAN WHO DOES (FEB. 2019)
8. NATURAL ♡ (FEB. 2019)
9. LEAVIN' CLEVELAND (MAR. 2019)
10. I'M CRAZY :) (MAR. 2019)
11. BETTER THE FIRST TIME (APRIL 2019)

WRITTEN + SANG BY: Megan Katarina
PRODUCED BY: JARED ANDERSON

The original handwritten back cover of the 2020 album, *To Be Honest*.

CREATURE OF PASSION

Written December 2017

Don't try to speak sense
Or talk logic and ration
If you are talking
To a creature of passion

Don't tally the numbers
And divvy them up
Creatures of passion
Don't make math of love

Those who fear the vulnerable
Will call these creatures beasts
But those who feel the world
Will deem them a masterpiece

And ones with closed minds
Will think these creatures fools
Because they don't swim
Inside of shallow pools

But they do not care
If they're judged bad or good
All they desire
Is to be understood

And I hear these days
Indifference is in fashion
But I'd rather stay
A creature of passion

So trust me, when you fall
As we all will and do
You should pray a creature of passion
Chooses you

PLANS

Written December 2017

I painted my lips
Adorned rings on my hands
Looking for someone
To come share their plans

I compromised truth
And wore shame like a gown
Waiting for someone
To build my life around

For what better distraction
From my own messy self
Than to lose who I am
Inside somebody else?

In time, I found one
Then another, again
And made each the axis
To revolve my plans

And each time plans shattered
I lay devastated
Desperate to avoid
The chaos I created

Then finally, one day
The wreckage piled too high
I learned living for someone else
Was living a lie

Alone and afraid
And though silly, they seemed
I decided for once
To try chasing MY dreams

I nursed my own wounds
And set dates with myself
To speak with my pain
And just let it be felt

I began to move on
To my own sweet surprise
And with a new year
Even healing arrives

And love is still something
I don't understand
But I do know it's better
When I make my own plans

I THINK TOO MUCH

Written December 2017

I think too much
That's what they say
100 thoughts
For EVERY time of day

I observe the strangeness
In a season's ending
And behold life's peculiar
Ways of mending

I think too much
That's why I'm odd
And when I talk
My mind drifts off

I ponder the bitterness
In change
And marvel at its sweetness
All the same

I think too much
So they say my fate
Is to ponder and wrestle
The whole world's weight

I admit, they are right
Sometimes I'm engulfed
In problems
That aren't even my own to solve

My mind has a mind of its own
They believe
But I love my mind
And my mind loves me

I think too much
The world claims I'm cursed
But at the end of my worst
Are my best thought's birth

I think too much
But it doesn't bother me
For I wish to know the world
The way it knows me

And because I think too much
I've often considered
Is it I that thinks too much?
Or them, that thinks too little?

I think too much
Thats what they say
100 thoughts for EVERY time of day
I observe the strangeness in
endings
& behold life's peculiar ways
of mending
I think too much
Thats why I'm odd
When I talk
My mind drifts off
I ponder the bitterness in
change
& marvel at it's sweetness
all the same
I think too much
So they say my fate
Is to ponder & wrestle
The whole world's weight
I admit they are right
Sometimes I'm engulfed →

In problem's that aren't
mine
But I wish too solve
My mind of its own,
they believe
But I love my mind
& my mind loves me
I think too much
The world proclaims, I'm cursed
But at the end of my
worst thoughts,
Are my best ideas birth
I think too much
But that doesn't ho
B/c I wish to know the
world
Since like it knows me
I think too much
Ive often considered
Is it I that thinks too
much or is it
Them that thinks too
LITTLE

I THINK TOO MUCH

Once during a visit to Florida for Christmas, I went to the beach for some solo time at my favorite restaurant. After a walk in the sand, this poem came to me as I sat on a bench and watched a storm come in. I was thinking about all the times I have been made to feel like I am weak for overthinking. This poem is my response to such ignorance!

THE MIDDLE

Written December 2017

There is a place where no one stays
But everyone must go
A place everyone learns what they wish
They did not have to know

At the end of oblivion
And the start of change
There's a place we call "The Middle"
That is best known for its pain

I know I'm not the only one
Who's tried to skip this spot
Who could blame me?
It's the longest and the hardest of the lot

My first vain idea
Was to avoid it altogether
But staying at the start
Just left me feeling bored and tethered

Then I thought I'd venture on
But I'd run and do it fast
Until I tripped and fell upon
My pride, my guilt, my past

Afraid, I turned around
To find a shortcut through the weeds
But avoiding the laborious hike
Just forced me deeper in between

With open cuts and bruises
I decided to surrender
And though the climb was daunting
I did not deny its splendor

I began to learn myself
Inside the stillness of the dark
And heal a little quicker
With each scar that left its mark

Until one day when it'd been long
Since I let my life be ruled by fear
I wasn't even looking anymore
But I was here

That's the thing about the middle,
It's quite maddening, you see,
It will not deem you "ready"
Until you stop pretending to be

And though it'd be lovely to bypass
The place where hurt occurs
Where every statement is just a question
Of who you are and who you were

I wish not to regret the times
When life made me feel brittle
'Cause how would I have made it here
If I had skipped the middle?

Yes, how would I be who I am
If I had skipped the middle?

THE MIDDLE

In 2018, I wanted to write more poetry, so I bought a journal that was specifically labeled "Poetry and Prose." I was also prepping to release my album soon and I was planning to recite poetry on the album, so I wanted to get my chops up. The weeks leading up to this time were filled with angst and uncertainty. I truly felt I was in "The Middle," a place where I wasn't totally breaking down, but I wasn't yet reaching my full potential. This poem poured out one night.

Around this time, I joined a creative writing class on a whim. We were asked to bring our poetry to read and discuss with the group. I brought this poem because I felt it was one of my most profound. The leader of the class told me the poem was a great children's poem because it rhymed. I was absolutely floored by how she had missed the message of the poem and only focused on the format.

It's not her fault, rhyming poems have been discriminated against for years by academics because they are seen as "low brow" poetry. But the truth is all formats of poetry can be abused or made cheap, and all can be a vessel for a meaningful message!

At the end of the class, this older lady sitting next to me asked me quietly, "Do you mind if I take this poem with me? I really relate to it." That little spark of connection with a stranger lifted my spirits tremendously.

I think the sweet spot of craft is somewhere between me, a die-hard believer in following the muse, and the class teacher, a believer in following the format. But, I never went back to that creative writing class.

THE PRICE OF SIMPLICITY

Written January 2018

She tucks you into bed at night
And kisses you good day
She doesn't make you feel alive
But she makes you feel safe

You say you love her, and you do
Just not like you've loved before
Tell me, do you wish for chaos
Or is this what you live for?

Your thoughts don't wander off to me
Much to your own surprise
But the jewels of my memory
Lay buried in your deep desires

I don't long for simplicity
And you don't long for complex
So your heart's own passion for me
Left your mind completely vexed

Now you've chosen the easy path
In which the odds stay in your favor
Do you wonder if the choice you've made
Will satisfy you later?

She tucks you into bed at night
And wishes you sweet dreams
But when you close your eyes
I bet that it's not her you see

THE PRICE OF SIMPLICITY

When I was living in Nashville, a few months before releasing *Being Crazy Ain't For The Weak*, I was finishing up writing for the album. One night I was hanging out with a girlfriend and talking about the songs and the guy I wrote them about. I was still not over him, and she said, "Well, why don't we just look him up?" (Never a good idea.) So, we looked him up on Facebook and I saw that within a month after we broke up, he had gotten back with his ex and was engaged to her! I was absolutely blindsided. This guy who told me I was the only one for him and made me believe it just wasn't the right time for us to be together, immediately got back together with his ex after we broke up! Keep in mind, I was only twenty-one at this time so it was the end of the world. I was so upset I started shaking and I immediately wrote this poem.

The next day at a co-write, I showed up with my poem, hoping to write a song based off of it. We started writing something really heavy, because the feeling behind it was truly heavy. But then, my friend threw out the line, "You're just doing what's easy." And I said, "Stop what you're doing right now, because we're going to write a song called 'Doing What's Easy' and it's going to be funny!" And that is how my track "Doing What's Easy" came to be on my album *Being Crazy Ain't For The Weak*. It all started with this poem!

BRAVE HEART

Written January 2018; Recorded by Megan Katarina on album *Being Crazy Ain't For The Weak*, track 8

I blamed you
I named you
The cause of all my issues
I prayed to
Just hate you
But I could only miss you
All my friends dragged me out
I got drunk and cried in bars
I broke down called you up
Just to make a deeper scar

Believed the story that my life
would never change
That my chance at love was broken
and I'd never be the same but

When you tore me apart
You gave me a brave heart
I gave you everything
And I lost everything
Or so I thought
But if I'd never took a shot
And loved so hard
I'd never have a brave heart

You didn't play fair
But I was scared
To be myself without you
I wished to
Not miss you
But I did not know how to
Reckless is as reckless does
And reckless was better than blind
Nothin' to lose made me choose
To finally say what's on my mind

And do what I wanted
'cause I didn't care no more
But when I lost you
I found what I was made for

When you tore me apart
You gave me a brave heart
I gave you everything
And I lost everything
Or so I thought
But if I'd never took a shot
And loved so hard
I'd never have a brave heart

The end of the world was the
beginning of my destiny
You might've taken a piece
but I kept the best of me

When you tore me apart
You gave me a brave heart
I gave you everything
And I lost everything
Or so I thought
But if I'd never took a shot
And loved so hard
I'd never have a brave heart

Brave ♥ @1/2/...
megan
klau

I blamed you
I named you
the cause of all my issues
I prayed to
Just hate you
But I could only miss you
All my friends dragged
me out I got drunk
cried in bars
I broke down called you up
up ~~~~ just to make
a deeper scar
I believed the story
that to my life never
change
that my chance at love
was broken & Id never
be the same but

— CHORUS —

When you tore me apart
You gave me a brave ♥

You didn't play fair
But I was scared
to be myself w/o you
I wished to
Not miss you
But I did not know to

reckless is as reckless
does & reckless better
than kind
nothin to lose
Made me choose
to ~~~~ finally say whats
on my mind & do
what I wanted cause
I didnt care no more
But when I lost you
I found out what
I was made for

CHORUS

bridge
the end of the world
was the beginning of my
destiny
You mightve taken a piece
But the rest of me

BRAVE HEART

The story behind this song is different than most of my songs because it took months to write in a roundabout way. Usually my writing style is pretty quick and in the moment, but there is always the occasional outlier of a song that I sit on for months before it's done. This song started as a free write, then morphed into a poem called "Brave Heart" in my journal.

The reason it took weeks for me to write this song down is because I was so devoted to creating an album that was purely country, that I rejected this pop melody for so long before finally surrendering and writing it. As I've gotten older, I've drifted more to folk/pop because of the lack of opportunities for women in country music, among other reasons, but at that time, I thought I could spur a revolution in the genre.

When I finally wrote "Brave Heart," I played it for my friends and they loved it, but I hated it. I thought it was way too bubblegum and corny. Eventually none of us could get it out of our head and it became such an earworm that it would be stupid not to record.

It's now one of my favorite songs on the record for the true life story that it tells. I'm so grateful for all the reckless mistakes I've made in love that taught me how to be BRAVE.

WINGS

Written January 2018

Wings aren't made of feathers,
Wings are made of pain,
And if you wish to fly,
You first must face your doubt and shame,
So don't you wish away the scars,
Or regret the trying times,
Cause the very things that made you break,
Are the things that made you fly.

WINGS

If you're a fan of my music, you may have heard this poem before. This poem is the precursor to part two of *Being Crazy Ain't for the Weak*. I wanted to split my album into two parts, the darkness and the revelation. So I named part one, "Anchor," and part two, "Wings." Once I came up with the concept, I wrote two poems to sum up the story and precede the songs in each part. This is one of them.

Bein Crazy Aint 4 the Week

PT. 1 — ANCHOR

* 1. anchor → } order?
2. weak Moment ✓
2* 3. Hes seen me Naked →
. 4. Bein crazy aint for the weak
. 5. ~~I set you free~~ I set you free

Poetry ?? . %   ?

"Art should comfort the disturbed & disturb the comfort.

PT. 2 — WINGS

* 1. Its not you its me →
2* 2. ~~Predictable~~ ? better for me able
3. ~~flavors~~ • nothin to prove Brave heart
4. ✓ Rollin Stone flavors saved • im gettin drunk
* 5. ✓ & → Months' Sober • crazy too some thing never change

✓ Im gettin drunk ?

Take your broken

♡ & turn it into

ART !

This is the original album plan for *Being Crazy Ain't for the Weak*. I drew it up in my journal and then wrote the poetry preludes to "Wings" and "Anchor."

MAGIC

Written April 2018

It was magic
It truly was
I still believe that now

It was magic
Pure magic
I still do not know how

It was real
And even now
It still feels so sincere

And when you left
Just as I believed
The magic disappeared

It was magic
So sweet, it hurts
For me to remember

And I looked
For that magic
High and low since last December

It was magic
True and rare
Just too special to find

But to my surprise
One day I found
It lived inside my mind

It was magic
It still is
Oh, never did it leave

I thought that
When you left
I could no longer believe

But it was magic
Real magic
I still believe it now

I had it inside
All along
You simply were around

MAGIC

I love this poem because it's about stepping into your own power. I was looking back on all the "magical" memories of a past relationship and I had this realization that it was me who was creating the magic. I was the one who wanted to go on adventures, and get into conversation with random people, and find secret places. I was the one creating a special memory, and the other person was just there. So, if it was I who was creating the magic, then I can still have it on my own.

I feel like there is so much greatness & love within me & around me. There are so many who love & support me. Yet, there is a veil between me & them & I can't feel it all. I feel so cold. Isolation. Numbness. Fear. Inadequateness.

What is truth. — ?

Is it true that others are better than me?

I talk to people that appear to "have it all figured out" with such meekness & submission, & inconfidence of who I am & what I bring to this world.

Why do I do that?

Am I not fully worthy of being heard?

What is truth?

Perhaps the truth is that my voice is important.

My voice, the one I am so ashamed of, the one I am so afraid to use, the one I overuse, underuse, confuse...

My voice is here to tell truth.

The truth is what heals me, what heals others.

The truth is my only responsibility.

If I am not ready to tell it, then I will not speak. But I won't lie.

& I will always tell the truth.

I should be proud of this.

This is a journal page I wrote in the fall of 2018 a few months after the release of my album. The business puts lots of pressure on you to keep achieving, and often times of great success are followed by times of doubt and confusion.

DEPARTURE

I lived my life repetitively

So stagnant and so certain

In desperate desire

To let my eyes

Have a glimpse behind the curtain

In the shelter of protection

I thought danger to be my fate

The thrill of a risk

Too inspiring to resist

In my naïve youthful haste

I set out with starry eyes

To fall in love with places

What I didn't know

Was everywhere I'd go

I'd fall in love with faces

Adventures and romances

Were my heart's own deepest craving

Though actually

What they had to teach

Would be my means of saving

Youth is wasted on the young

The elders say with woe

But the quests and trials

Of the juvenile

Will be the wisdom of tomorrow!

Pictures from 2008 to present.

Freediving in mexico. Photograph by mike winkles.

INITIATION

An initiation can simply mean the beginning of something, but it can also mean an admission into an exclusive group or school of thought. In folklore, an initiation usually represents a time of growth, spurred by struggle and loss of innocence. The lifting of the veil from the eyes. The predecessor to redemption.

My earliest experience of initiation brings me back to my school years. I remember being in sixth grade, with my enormous rolling backpack and wacky sense of humor, literally skipping down the halls to class. I was bullied for my "weirdness" and had virtually no friends until I made it to eighth grade. Then I was taken under the wing of my popular childhood friend. She taught me to line my eyes, buy short shorts from Hollister, and even have my first kiss. I was so lonely and desperate to fit in at this point that I did whatever she said. It was around this time that I remember thinking in order to be liked, I need to be quiet, I need to be pretty, and I need to hide who I really am. This became my mantra throughout the next five years. It led me to a breaking point in high school where I developed a binge eating disorder and drank to excess often. I quit music for most of high school because I was so embarrassed that I was different.

I spent so much time in my teens trying to fit in that I became severely depressed and developed social anxiety. This did improve exponentially after I graduated, but that peace became short-lived when I moved to Nashville at age twenty-one. I was told by music execs and songwriting peers that my music wasn't commercial enough, my sound is "too girly" (what does that mean?), and I need to use smaller words for my audience. It was such a boy's club, full of city guys pretending to be country guys trying to write the best song they could about something they knew nothing about. I watched what others did to get ahead and I knew it would never align with my character. I felt alone and misunderstood. So what did I do? Well, I tried to fit in of course!

The problem with "fitting in" is that you are holding pieces of yourself captive because the societal norms have deemed them ugly or inconvenient. Not only does society not accept these parts of you, but you don't. To numb the pain of not accepting myself, I had two preferred drugs: television and food. For years, I abused them to an alarming degree. I was constantly thinking about food and eating until I felt sick. Netflix was always playing in the background. This was how I would distract myself because I couldn't face reality. I did learn to heal these addictions, and you'll read about that in this chapter. But they were born of my trying to self-suppress to belong.

In this period of my life, I shifted the focus of my creations to reflecting on the past. As kids we see the world through "rose-colored glasses," and our brains aren't yet developed enough to understand the nuances and evils of our world. You saw a lot of that in my last chapter. I realized that because I began my career at such an early age, I became frozen in that child's mindset for a long time, hungry for approval and acceptance. I suffered more because I was too trusting and overly devastated when disappointed. In my last chapter, I told you that I have a tendency to run from my problems and you've now learned some of my favorite ways of being an escape artist: love, travel, food, television. (Probably in that order too.) But eventually it all caught up to me and I realized I had to face these issues. And in order to face them, I had to face my past.

This leads me to the collection you will read in this chapter, a series of poems, lyrics, and stories from the years 2018–2020, or ages twenty-two to twenty-three. The largest lesson I learned from this series of hard initiations into my womanhood is that there is a gigantic price to pay for not being your true self. I know this more than anyone. And I prefer to pay the other price. The one you pay for being yourself. Sometimes, that can be painful. Vulnerability makes others uncomfortable, and some people would rather criticize it than meet it with their own.

But for me personally, creating art from a place of honesty has been the most effective remedy to healing my past and bringing me into the present. My greatest teacher has always been my aching heart. And with every heartbreak I've learned to let go of my childlike idealizations and slowly embrace what it means to love and live as my true self. Pain hides in places we would never think to look, until it has festered and grown into something larger and more difficult to discern. And so, it's imperative to have courage. The courage to love the parts of yourself that you hate. The courage to forgive. And the courage to be who you really are.

Don't

apologize for who

Don't who apologize for you are

who apologize for you are.

Don't you are apologize for who

healing starts here.

WAVES

Written June 2018

I used to be afraid of waves
Since I was a child
Changing and unstoppable
I thought them much too wild

Although I've always loved the feel
Of sand gripping my feet
I'd never let those feet step past
Three or four feet deep

Maybe because when I was six
The water overtook me
I remember how the tumble to the shore
Forever shook me

Petrified and soaking wet
Afraid to suffocate
Never would I hold my breath
Again, beneath a wave

Sometimes when I'm overwhelmed
And feeling powerless
I dream that a tsunami
Sweeps me to my death

Am I afraid of drowning?
I've always claimed to be

Or am I afraid of surrender
To the wind, the earth, the sea

There are very little things
In this life that I can control
Let alone the moon and sun's
Gravitational pull

I've always tried to stand my ground
To fight and dodge the waves
Never going with them
Hearing what they have to say

But I dove in yesterday
Deeper than I've ever gone
I floated and I played and wished
That time would not move on

When I patted dry my face
I smiled at the ocean
Adoring how it ebbed and flowed
But stayed rooted in motion

Surrender, I thought
To the things that always change
Maybe my new friends, the waves
Weren't the reason I was afraid

WAVES

This entire poem is a true story. I spent the summer of 2018 playing shows at beaches in Florida. Once, on break during a show, I decided to walk across the street and into the waves. I had my bathing suit on under my clothes and made the silly decision to just jump in! I had such a profound experience swimming and floating in the waves that I wrote this poem about it.

Freediving in mexico. Photograph by mike winkles.

VESSEL

Written June 2018

My sweet two feet
Take me from
Point A to B
They point, they flex
They dance, they flee
Have I told you yet?
I love you, feet

My lovely legs
Are strong and brave
They take me places even when I'm afraid
The muscular structure
Holds me up
Lets me play
I love you, legs

My sweet stomach
Endures much abuse
I call it names
I fill it with food
But its ebbs and flows
Should be listened to
I love you, stomach

My chest protects
My heart and lungs
It stands me straight
To fill me up
With oxygen
While I live and rest
I love you, chest

My ambitious arms
I tend to grab
But they are much more

Than muscle and fat
They hold my nieces
They protect me from harm
I love you, arms

My beautiful hands
Most forgotten of all
They touch, they comfort
They break my falls
They draw sweet messages
In the sand
I love you, hands

My precious head
With my busy brain
My face to express
My thoughts to proclaim
It's what makes me, me
May I never forget
I love you, head.

This is a love note
To thank you for all
The work you devote
To keep me standing tall
Forgive my complaining, crying, taunting
This is my peace offering
I love you, body

Now I will pray
I pray that I may
No longer insult, oppose, or betray
I will love with intensity instead of wrestle
My own, unique, functional, lovely

VESSEL.

VESSEL

I remember the exact moment my eating disorder began. When I was a freshman in high school, I was on the varsity dance team and trying everything in my power to be cool and get male attention. The girls on the dance team weren't very kind and I had a leg injury so I wasn't able to fully dance at the time. After a particularly grueling practice, we had gotten these big tubs of cookie dough to sell as a fundraiser. I was the last one in the room. I opened the tub of cookie dough, and suddenly I couldn't stop eating it.

The rest of my high school experience was spent hiding cereal boxes and empty ice cream tubs in my room. My parents did not understand why I couldn't just "stop eating." I gained 40 pounds. I tried diets that would just end two days later with a huge binge. I was teased for being chubby, but bingeing was the only way I knew how to deal with my big emotions. It created a cycle of self-destruction: binge, feel terrible, go out to a party or something social to feel better, embarrass myself, binge to feel better, repeat. Eating was my drug.

My heart breaks for my younger self. Even as I lost the weight and eventually healed my disorder almost a decade later, for so long I saw myself as this undesirable girl. I believed myself to be repulsive. I had to heal this thought in therapy, put myself in her shoes to feel empathy for her instead of hatred and disgust. It was not easy for me, but I know that ultimately what healed my binge eating disorder was surrounding myself with people who loved me for me, expressing my emotions in healthy ways, and most importantly, forgiving and relating to my past self. Not just once, but many times. I can now honestly tell you that I have a very positive relationship with my body. I'm grateful that I have a living, working body, and I'm so remorseful for all the abuse I've put it through. This is my love letter to my body.

SLOW

Written June 2018

There's nothing wrong
With moving slow
Biding, biding, biding

Float and play
Ride the wave,
Not fighting, fighting, fighting

There's no doubt
Life's all about,
Timing, timing, timing

But time is wise
It moves despite
Your striving, striving, striving

And you'll still go
If you go slow
Thriving, thriving, thriving!

TIME (ON THIS DAY)

Written June 2018

On this day, two years ago
My hands would shake
My blood run cold
Another day of hoping you won't leave
Living with love on the rocks
Wasn't much living at all
But you were the only thing
That I believed

On this day, one year ago
I didn't have your hand to hold
But you were still the ruler
Of my mind
Sometimes happy, sometimes sad
I knew my true life had began
If only I could stop
Looking behind

On this day, six months ago
In a brand-new place
And a sweet new home
I realized it'd been days
Since you crossed my thoughts
A wound not closed but healing well
Heart awakened and a story to tell
From a fight that never needed
To be fought

On this day, three months ago
Life told me she loved me so
I finally loved something
That loved me back
I told our story, thought of you
Then let it go into the blue
Done holding on
To what I never had

On this day, last weekend,
Pain, my old familiar friend
Reminded me
Of what I used to have
I simply yelled into the bay
"Look at who I am today!"
Would I be this
If you had come back?

On this day
I woke up late
Stretched my body lovingly
And bowed to God because I am alive
My smiling eyes
My sun-kissed skin
My inspiration and chagrin
Result of the only true healer:

Time.

TIME (ON THIS DAY)

I love this poem because it's a timeline of healing. Often, I'll look at the time and think to myself, "At this time, twenty-four hours ago, I was _____" or "At this time, in six hours, I'll be _____." Time fascinates me. During the time that I wrote the album *Being Crazy Ain't for the Weak*, it was hard to look at those Facebook "Memories" that pop up and tell you where you were one year ago. But once I finally started healing, it became easier and easier to look at the past without despair, which inspired this reflection on the beautiful way that time heals.

SAND

Written July 2018

I feel the sand between my toes
I taste the cold salt air
I feel the wind upon my nose
I remember what we did here

We stripped down to just skin
And jumped into the sea
And when the sea was too cool
We crashed that pool without a key

Your hands traced my body
Like an expensive piece of art
I saw your eyes behold me
As they wished we'd never part

Tonight is cold and foggy
And I'd freeze if I went in
Funny how being back where
Brings you to back when

I cannot see the moon tonight
I wonder if you can
But I bet you that I'm on your mind
Next time you touch this sand

SAND

When I was a teenager still living in central Florida, most of my early romances were set on the beach. A few years later while living in Nashville, I came home to visit and went to the beach. All the memories came rushing back and I had to sit down in the sand and write this one.

ACCEPTANCE

Written August 2018

The secret to freedom

And the remedy to pain

Is knowing

Endings
and
Beginnings

are truly the same.

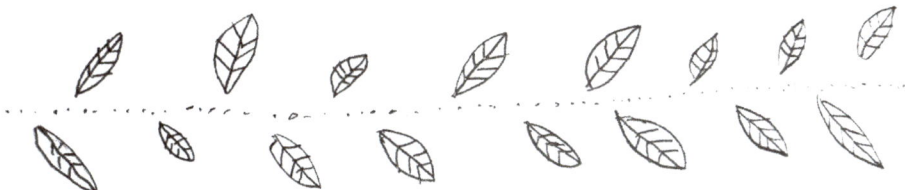

BRIDGES WORTH BURNING

Written September 2018; Recorded by Megan Katarina on album *To Be Honest*, track 4

I hate going back to my hometown
Seeing all the boys that still hang around
I hate running into old friends
And acting like there's common ground

I hate talking to fill space
I don't want to succeed by playing a game
I think I keep my pride in line
But some things ain't worth compromise

I'd rather have a real friend than a million people patting my back
I'd rather cry at home alone than to beg for the wrong one back
It ain't worth the time it takes to smile and pretend
And some lessons are worth learning
But some bridges are worth burning

I've spent years ignoring facts
Waking up in the beds of ghosts from the past
But what am I losing if I don't want it back
Whose face am I saving if I'm wearing a mask

I'd rather have a real friend than a million people patting my back
I'd rather cry at home alone than to beg for the wrong one back
It ain't worth the time it takes to smile and pretend
And some lessons are worth learning
But some bridges are worth burning

What friend is a friend that I don't want to have
For the sake of connection or not looking bad
If I don't mean what I say, it ain't a conversation
Who I am is more important than my reputation

I'd rather have a real friend than a million people patting my back
I'd rather cry at home alone than to beg for the wrong one back
It ain't worth the time it takes to smile and pretend
And some lessons are worth learning
But some bridges are worth burning

HEALING

Written October 2018

What is a wound
An inconvenience
A heavy, grueling pain?

Is a wound
What keeps us rooted
In that old familiar pain?

Is a wound
The reason why
We can't smile or succeed?

Or is a wound
An excuse for
That what lies beneath?

Is a wound
A teacher
That shows us who we are?

Why we're here
What we know
And how we got this far?

Is a wound
A blessing?
Some say it should be

It gives us a story
And shows us
What we're here to teach

Is a wound
An unfortunate
Side effect of being alive?

Or is a wound
A precious gift?
Only you decide.

MY BODY IS A VESSEL FOR RECEIVING... Loving Energy

HELLO GOD

Written November 2018

Hello God
How do you do?
Am I wise to speak with you?
Or am I only talking to myself?

Hello God
Please bring me love
Blue skies and sunshine up above
And for my family, please bring good
health

Hello God
Why is life pain?
Is there a point, or am I insane?
A victim to my mortal circumstance?

Hello God
It's me again
Will these questions ever end?
Am I a fool to try to understand?

Hello God
We spoke today
A stranger's face in a warm cafe
I recognized you in their joyful laugh

Hello God,
We meet again
In my mirror's reflection
Now I do not wonder where you're at

Hello God
No complaints today
No questions or requests to pray
Since I've finally realized You. Are.
Love.

Hello God
Life is not fair
I know it's true and I don't care
But I am yours and I'm alive
Today that is enough.

I'M READY TO BE LOVED

Written November 2018; Recorded by Megan Katarina on album *To Be Honest*, track 5

I've faced all my demons
I fought them with courage and truth
Mistakes that I've blamed others for
I've owned up to those too

I say sorry when I'm wrong
I'm happy on my own
I've even made peace with my pride
And honestly I'm better than fine

But I'm ready to be loved
I don't mean that this ain't enough
I've faced the facts
And loosened my grasp
I know that I cannot go back
But I'm ready to be loved
Oh I'm ready to be loved

I know I've done things
That have kept me from it in the past
But now I know love is a force that
I can't force to do what I ask

I've rushed it and I've missed it
For a while I was addicted
It refuses to be used, I see
But I bet love would do good using me

But I'm ready to be loved
I don't mean that this ain't enough
I've faced the facts
And loosened my grasp
I know that I cannot go back
But I'm ready to be loved
Oh I'm ready to be loved

I know what it is 'cause I know what it isn't
And I want to have it 'cause I want to give it
I am not a master I am a defender
Love, if you're listening, I surrender

But I'm ready to be loved
I don't mean that this ain't enough
I've faced the facts
And loosened my grasp
I know that I cannot go back
But I'm ready to be loved
Oh I'm ready to be loved

IM READY TO BE LOVED
© megan klauk 11/2

Ive faced all my demons
I fought them with courage
& truth
mistakes that Ive blamed
others for Ive owned up to
those too
I say sorry when I'm
wrong I'm ⟨CURIOUS⟩ ... in my own ... made peace w/my life
... honestly while ... life is better than fine

But I'm ready to be loved
I don't mean that this aint
enough
& Ive faced the facts
& loosened the grasp
I know that I can not
go back
But I'm ready to
be loved

I know I did things
that @ kept me from love
in the past
But I've been to hell with
myself to make sure I am my best

I'M READY TO BE LOVED

These are the lyrics of a song I wrote when I was about twenty-two years old. I felt for a long time that I was the reason why I hadn't found a relationship that stuck yet. So, I did everything I could to heal myself, but not for the right reasons. I did it with the goal of being in a healthy long-term relationship. That's not a bad goal to have, but I wish that when I was younger I would've understood that I need to do it for me, to be happy in my own company.

Around the time I wrote this, I just had this general feeling of impatience and anticipation, like, "Okay, I've done all I need to do. I'll take my happily ever after now!" And I wrote this song about that . . . about being so ready for love.

THE COST OF WORDS

Written November 2018

What if words were a currency
And not a means to an end
So that we'd have to mean it
Before we called someone "my love" or "my friend"

We'd pick them up on the way home
A list in a grocery store
We'd have to feel them first to know
Which words that we need more

We'd barter at the market
And choose each phrase with thought and caring
For only millionaires can afford
To recite the dictionary

A nickel for "How are you doing"
A penny for a lie: "Doing well"
But no one would waste their money
On stories they didn't care to tell

"I love you" would cost the highest price
So that only a fool wouldn't mean it
Gossip and small talk, a frivolous splurge
And we would only pray if we believe it

Perhaps those who can't afford small talk
Would be the happiest of all
For they would speak with a touch, a look,
And all the ways that words fall

To communicate simply by speaking
Often leaves much to be desired
For I often think the value of a statement
Would rise if the cost to speak was higher

If talking was part of the budget
I bet talk would never be cheap
For only the rich and the foolish
Would craft sentences they don't believe

Maybe love would be deeper
Maybe we would trust what we've heard
If there was a pension on promises
And we all knew the cost of our words

SOMEDAY'S COMIN' SOMEDAY

Written November 2018; Recorded by Megan Katarina on album *To Be Honest*, track 6

Someday I'm gonna have a house
Nobody knockin' on the bathroom door and yellin' get out
Someday I'll have a truck that runs
And I'll drive to the store without a maintenance light turning on

Someday I'll have a dog
And the dog will have a couch
Someday I won't be afraid to check my bank account

Someday's comin' someday
It don't matter how many heartaches it takes
If the world keeps spinnin' and I keep my faith
I know someday's comin' someday hey

Someday I'll sleep ten hours a night
And I'll lay my head in a bed that ain't twin sized
Someday I'll have a love that's true
And I'll know why the past had to do what it had to do

I won't cook dinner in a microwave
Or forget to lock my door
I know a little bit but I know someday I'm gonna know a little bit more

Someday's comin' someday
It don't matter how many heartaches it takes
If the world keeps spinnin' and I keep my faith
I know someday's comin' someday hey

Someday in hindsight I'll connect the dots I see
From the hard times that led me to the place I'm meant to be
And I'll miss the times I didn't know if I'd be okay
But I'll be okay, someday

Someday's comin' someday
It don't matter how many heartaches it takes
If the world keeps spinnin' and I keep my faith
I know someday's comin' someday hey

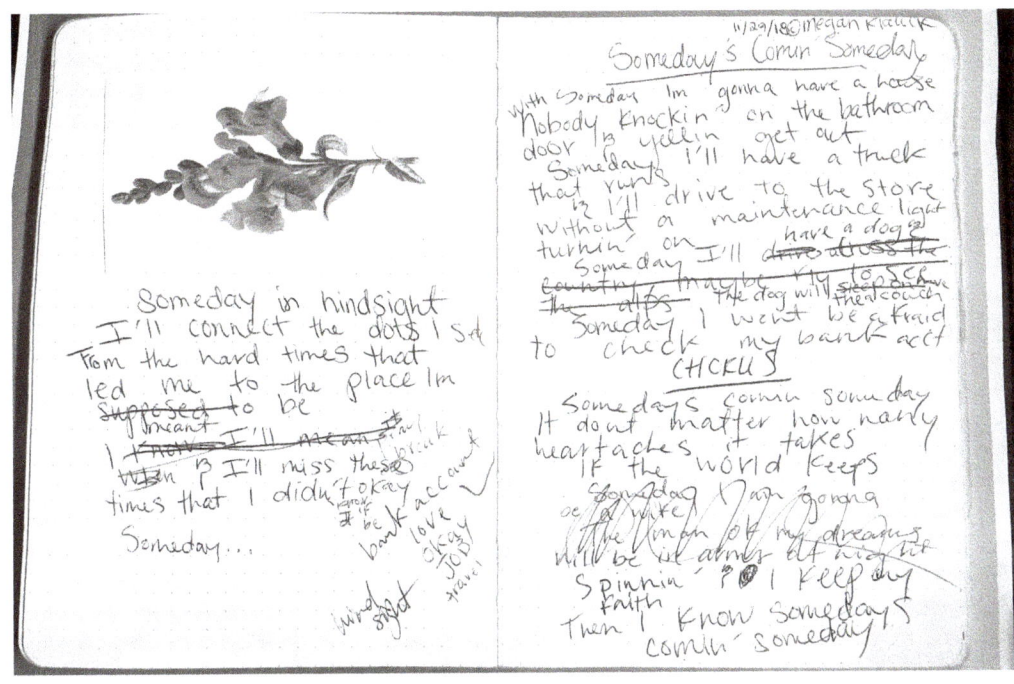

SOMEDAY'S COMIN' SOMEDAY

When I lived in Nashville I booked a weekly writer's room for myself every Wednesday. When I wrote this song, it was around November, and I was planning to go home to Florida for Christmas and play a lot of shows. I was counting on this for my income. One of the venues I had booked a lot of dates with called me one Tuesday night, canceled half of my shows, and docked my pay in half for the rest. I was distraught, and because I didn't have a contract, there was really nothing I could do. I was sitting in my car worrying about money, feeling like nothing could go right. I almost didn't go to the writer's room the next day because I felt I was too stressed to be creative. But I decided I'd go anyway.

Predictably, I spent the entire three hours just calling venues instead of writing and trying to suffice for that lost income. BUT, at the very end of the session, the words, "Someday's Comin' Someday" popped into my head. I wrote it down and let it float around my subconscious all week. Then, the next Wednesday, I showed up to the writer's room and immediately wrote this song. At first I thought this song was too silly and cheeky to perform at shows. But, once I started playing it out, I realized it was a good one to record, because people were relating to the true story, and seeing their own story within it.

CLEAN SLATE

Written December 2018

Funny that a diary
Costs less than a book that's written

For with the book
You can't make up the end or the beginning

Though I do love fairytales
And for a mystery novel, I'd pay

It could never be more valuable
Than the turn of a fresh new page

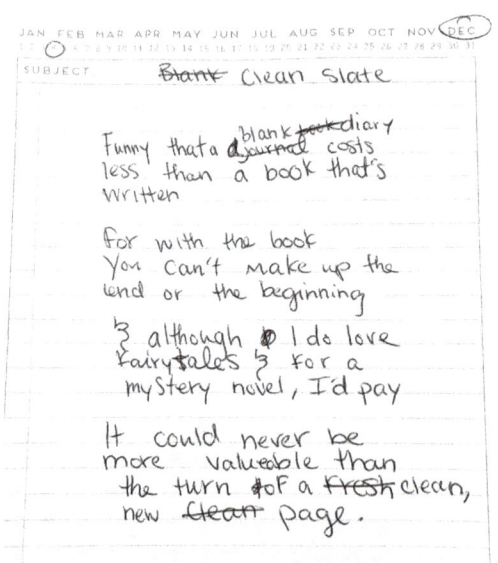

CLEAN SLATE

I used to spend the majority of my waking hours in Barnes & Noble, reading books, buying planners, but most importantly, checking out the new journals. Have you ever noticed how damn expensive those things are? I got the idea for this poem in the bookstore after thinking about the fact that I could buy a book for the same price as a journal with blank pages. But, I suppose, it's what you fill the pages with that creates the value.

LET IT BE WHAT IT IS

Written January 2019

Let it be what it is
Not what you make it
Before the passing of time
Swoops in to take it

Give thanks for the good
Not regrets for the bad
Before the present
Inevitably runs home to the past

Let it be ugly
Let it be real
For if you fake it
You'll never get to know how it feels

The moments in life
I cherish in full
Are always the ones
I forgot to control

Put trust in the world
To make moments of wonder
It's got millions of years
On your max of one hundred

Our time will come
So right now we should take it
Let it be what it is
Not what you make it

HONEST

Written May 2019

I felt it,
I wrote it,
I sang it,

They heard me.

Sometimes I feel
They don't even
Deserve me.

It's not that I'm better,
I'm not righteous,
Not pompous,

It's just, who has the guts

To be this goddamn
Honest?

HONEST

This is something I scribbled in my journal after a crappy show in Nashville. I felt like people in charge of booking venues often write me off because they see my vulnerable way of interacting with the crowd as weak or unprofessional. They are wrong, of course, but they are the ones in charge. This is frustrating. It's frustrating to play a song you wrote on your bedroom floor in a pivotal moment of your life for a crowd that pays no attention. And it's frustrating to be treated like you're a disposable entertainer when your message feels unique and meaningful to you. I don't think I'm the world's best writer or performer, but I believe that my message is authentic. Shouldn't that count for something?

BREAK MY HEART

Written June 2019

It was his mind, it was your eyes
I will hold on to whatever I can find, mhm
Blame it on the drink, blame it on the joke
My rearview mirror's the only ones without smoke, mhm

And every love feels different from the others
Until it just becomes one of the rest
I always say I won't get my hopes up
But here I am again givin' my best

It ain't the first time or the last
But every time hurts just as bad
I still like to hear them say forever
Even though I know better
I know better than that
And it might take a week or two
To glue the broken parts
But soon I won't remember you
And I'll find a brand-new guy to break my heart

Here I go again, carried away
Should listen to my friends, but I don't listen till it's too late, mhm
Is love just blind or am I blind girl
Makin' every man the start and end of my world mhm

Love makes me feel like I am immortal
Until I find myself six feet below
I want so badly for you to be the one
But I've wanted it with someone else before so how could I know

It ain't the first time or the last
But every time hurts just as bad
I still like to hear them say forever
Even though I know better
I know better than that
And I wonder if and when

There won't be an end to every start
When history repeats and
I still need a brand-new guy to break my heart

And another one to put it back together
And I'll hang onto every word he's saying
And when the fall don't land me back in love
And I just end up landing on the pavement

It ain't the first time or the last
But every time hurts just as bad
I still like to hear them say forever
Even though I know better
I know better than that
How do I even trust myself
To let down this old guard
When every time I do
I end up with a brand-new guy to break my heart

MAN WHO DOES

Written February 2019; Recorded by Megan Katarina on album *To Be Honest*, track 7

I loved a man who talked about the way he loved me so
I loved a man who talked about the things that I don't know
I loved a man who told me what our future would hold
I thought all their promises could stand their weight in gold
I remember all I've heard
But now I want more than words

I want a man who does
What he says he'll do
Puts the weight to the words cause he means them too
Then I ain't trying to figure out how he ain't what he never was
I want a man who does
Really see it through
Doesn't have to be grand, just has to be true
So when I think of love I can finally think of trust
I don't want a man who talks
I want a man who does

When it comes to my heart every word I say I mean
I guess that's why I've always been so quick to just believe
But the truth is just what's true in the moment and that's nobody's fault
Well I think I've wrestled with expired truths for long enough
So when you say eternally
Baby show me what you mean

I want a man who does
What he says he'll do
Puts the weight to the words cause he means them too
Then I ain't trying to figure out how he ain't what he never was
I want a man who does
Really see it through
Doesn't have to be grand, just has to be true
So when I think of love I can finally think of trust
I don't want a man who talks
I want a man who does

I have loved the leavers, the deceivers, the believers
But now I see they're all the same
I have seen the better, the forever, turn to never
With no one but me to blame
And I don't know if I still even believe in love
But I want a man who does

I want a man who does
What he says he'll do
Puts the weight to the words cause he means them too
Then I ain't trying to figure out how he ain't what he never was
I want a man who does
Really see it through
Doesn't have to be grand, just has to be true
So when I think of love I can finally think of trust
I don't want a man who talks
I want a man who does

MAN WHO DOES

I've included the phone note that led to this song from my album *To Be Honest* because it unveils a bit of the process to you. This song started out as a feeling that I was trying to convey in words, but I couldn't quite figure out how. Isn't that what's so beautiful about art? It's often a translation of what our heart is telling us into human language.

I've always taken people's words very seriously, because I mean everything I say. If I make you a promise, I'll follow through. If I give you a compliment, I'm sincere. It took way too long for me to realize that not everyone means what they say. Sadly, I think that's a part of shedding your innocence and becoming an adult.

So, at first, I had written this song's hook as "I don't want a man who talks, I want a man who listens." But, it didn't seem right.

In further reflecting on all my past relationships, I realized so much of what I mourned was the future and promises we discussed. Things that were never really real. This song is a humble declaration of a new chapter. The chapter of love in action, not words.

I want a man who listens
I loved a man who talked about the way he loves me so
I loved a man who talked about the things that I don't know
I loved a man who talked about the future that would never come

I loved a man who talked about beautiful I am
Told me I'm amazing every

Now I know what I didn't know before
That promises are promises and sometimes nothing more
All this time I've been trying to find what's missin
I love a man who talks
But I wanna love a man who listens

This is the original phone note from when I first got the
idea for man who does. I jotted down these thoughts
and let them sit in the phone note until I revisited
and refined the idea into "man who Does."

THE SUN

Written July 2019

The sun's been setting all day long
Ever since it started burning
The sun has stayed ever the same
We're the ones who keep on turning

THE SUN

When I was on tour in 2019, I stopped to camp at a national park on my bucket list called Mesa Verde. It was late in the day and after setting up my tent and hiking around, I wanted to see the sunset. I found this hike to a viewpoint, but the sun was setting in like five minutes, so I ran as fast as I could up the hill and found a clearing to watch the end of the sunset. That's when these words came to my mind. A few years later, I wrote the poem "Sun Settling," which is like an elaborated version of this little rhyme.

WRITER'S ACHE

Written July 2019

This world is so big
I acknowledge it every day
Every beautiful detail
I observe

Sometimes
It fills me

But in being the constant
Observer,
Acknowledger,
I feel, also
excluded.

Seems like I'm always waiting on food when I journaled. I'm at fig tree cafe in San Diego. Last night was my last show here at Tin Roof. It went great ß the crowd was loving. I sold 4 CD= I'm sitting here ∅with my coffee watching these adorable little birds. I wonder why people think it's wierd to eat alone. It's actually way better than eating with people. ~~You can taste~~ your __food__! and people watch! I'm gonna go to La Jolla ß the lighthouse today ⅋ MAYBE hit the zoo after. I'm so exhausted. I'm so home__sick__. But I'm so close to being done.

TODAYS MANTRA

- I am safe -

A journal page written during my cross-country house concert tour in the summer of 2019.

8/29/19

Sitting at Galley Grill, my favorite) spot :) Last night I played my show at Looe Key Tiki bar & it went well. The summary of yesterday is that I just woke up EARLY 6am, barely slept :: & drove to the Keys. I had a fairly neutral, nice day, but was a little mentally exhausted by the time I got to the lower keys & my favorite spot to paddle in Islamorada was blocked off so I paddled at this not nearly as great spot before Big Pine & the wind was RIPPING! It was hard, stressful, & not super enjoyable. So then I checked into the "cabin" shack I got in Big Pine & it's actually awesome. Super primitive. I took a shower in the "outhouse" w/ a screen view of the mangroves. It was lovely! Then played the gig & pretty much no one I invited showed up, except for one of my Instagram followers & Kendall, the captain. And this girl I met at Kiki's a few months ago, who follows my music

A journal entry written on tour in the Florida Keys in August 2019.

TO LIVE

Written August 2019

When it's all over
I do not want to say:

That I lived carefully,
fearfully,
catching small glimpses
but staying wrapped
in comfort,
oblivion,
distraction

When it's all over
I want to say:

I saw life fully
That I chased it
Looked into its eyes
only to learn it
had its arms around me all along

But I had to be terrified,
wounded grotesquely,
risk stupidly,
face truth with bravery
before the veil would fall.

Yes, I had to be willing
To appear foolish
and make colossal mistakes

To say: I am willing to risk my life at the price of experiencing this world
(love, hate grief, wonder, confusion, joy, awe, embarrassment
in its entirety)

I will know I've lived
by all the deaths within me
followed by rebirth,
made possible by courage.

TO LIVE

When I was on tour in 2019, my last stop was a house concert in the middle of the country. There were some people I knew there that had been following me on Facebook. It was a really strange night.

After touring for about five months altogether—up to Maine and back to Tennessee, and then to Portland, through California, and across the Midwest back to Tennessee—I had done A LOT. There were some amazing house concerts and some flops. There were some really sweet days off camping in national parks, and some days where I just wished to be home and cried myself to sleep. It wasn't easy, but it was a major achievement for me personally, and I was excited to be playing one last show and then getting the hell out of dodge!

But this group of people didn't greet me like attendees usually do. Half of them ignored me, and the other half said really weird things to me like, "Wow, I can't believe you're still alive!" And though it was a great time with great people, I got the feeling that some of the people there were afraid to get out of their comfort zone, therefore seeing me get out of my own comfort zone made them, well, uncomfortable. It's not that they didn't enjoy the show. It's not that they weren't kind. It's just that many of them were really fearful people and they projected that fear onto me.

Now that a few years have gone by, I look back on that experience and I'm glad that I can play for people in places that I don't feel completely at home and make them think about things they don't normally think about. I see that as a responsibility and a huge gift that I can reach out to people with my art. But, three years ago, in that moment, I just felt unappreciated and generally weirded out. I went home and angrily wrote this in my journal.

We all get comfortable with what we surround ourselves with and tend to judge anything different; it's human nature. When I play house concerts, I'm stepping in the middle of that, and I expect to be misunderstood by some, but maybe one thing that I say sticks with someone and gives them courage to follow their heart. To live. And for that, I will keep doing this job, over and over again.

8/31 Buena
Vista, Co

Today I left Mesa Verde & stopped in Durango for coffee & work. Then I deposited my cash (2500, hallelujah!) & tried to get @ my nails done but apparently everyone makes appointments out West & so I just headed to Buena Vista. I love this town! One of my faves in Co. I got a camp right on the river & I can't wait for it to sing me to sleep ♡

A journal page written during my cross-country
house concert tour in the summer of 2019.

A BIBLIOPHILE'S LAMENT

Written September 2019

I wander through the lines,
Skipping, pausing, scanning,
My hands touch the spines,
As if touching a lover...

Letting each one know they matter,
Invigorated with energy,
Excited at the fact that I can never stop learning,

Then sadness—
Because I can never read them all.

WORK OF ART

Written September 2019

Honey, what they say is true
I've been to heaven and back,
And hell on earth is losing something
You thought you'd always have

Baby, you can look,
Go on, look long and hard,
Here are my demons
Here are my scars

And here's all the wrong I've done
That I can never take back

In my chest are pieces of a broken heart
But baby broken pieces still make a work of art

A mosaic out of pain and fear
A creation to show how I got here
Which way I turned
Where I was burned
Of what I learned, of what I learned

Only I get to decide what I choose to do
With this colored past
You can see prisms of light or draw blood
With a piece of broken glass

I don't regret it, no
What I've been through
It led me to wisdom
It led me to you

And I've never known a life
As simple as white and black

Yeah, I have chipped some edges making it this far,
But baby broken pieces still make a work of art

A mosaic out of pain and fear
A creation to show how I got here
Which way I turned
Where I was burned
Of what I learned, of what I learned

To be broken is
To be human
Please forgive me if
I don't know what I'm doing
To be brave is
To be honest
I might've changed this heart
But I never lost it, no I never lost it

And I know life ain't good if it ain't sometimes hard
'Cause baby broken pieces still make

A gorgeous glass pane
Of experience
The times I prayed and
The times that I gave up
When I felt tough
When I felt easy to break
If I'm being honest
They always felt the same yeah

A mosaic out of pain and fear
A creation to show how I got here
Which way I turned
Where I was burned
Of what I learned, of what I learned

I can never put together all these broken parts
But baby broken pieces still make a work of art

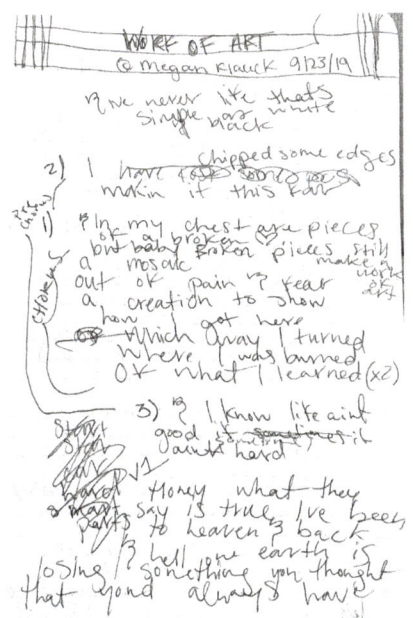

WORK OF ART

I have this habit of choosing significant others that are the exact opposite of me. I'm so flighty and emotionally driven that it feels great to be with someone who's grounded and logical. One of my old boyfriends and I got into an argument once and he sort of minimized the way I process emotions because he didn't understand. I was upset and I wanted to explain to him that even though there are downsides to being sensitive and artistic, it makes me who I am. Everything that has hurt me, formed me, and made me everything I am today. You can't have the good without the bad, otherwise you wouldn't know just how good it is.

oh hey, inner wisdom   10/24/20

Although there are many who will convince you it is, please know, it is not a crime to be complex. I refuse to make myself convenient by hiding my multitudes. I will take others as they are & hope they do the same for me.

A journal page from 2020.

DEPTH

Written January 2020

I spent day after tiring day
Giving my all to explain
The vastness of myself to you
But still you never had a clue

I blamed myself, for I'm too complex
And you'd rather blame than self-reflect
So, it was I who was accused
Condemned inside your box with you

Square peg, round hole situation
Fastened chains to my imagination
My emotions in bottles on shelves
You weren't to be bothered with what I saw and felt

But was it a crime? I wasn't so sure
That I felt life just a little bit more
And so, not serving my sentence, I left
I, found guilty, of having depth

Photograph taken by Emily Richo.

INITIATION

I remember the day I learned
How easy it is to tell a lie
I remember the day I learned
That life will mostly be goodbyes
I recall each crack in my heart
That made it beat in disarray
And I remember the time
My heart told my mind,
"It's more beautiful this way."

Photos from my house concerts

RETURN

I have a tattoo on my left arm that says, *"Dadme La Muerte Que Me Falta."* It's old Spanish for "Give me the death I need." It's a line from a poem by Mexican mystic poet Rosario Castellanos that stuck with me ever since I read it. I was so proud of this tattoo when I first received it, for it was my declaration of embracing change and surrendering to whatever comes my way. But when people started asking about it, they looked at me with confusion or disgust, wondering why I would ask for death. "Do you want to die?" some would ask, usually drunk at a show I was playing. I got so frustrated with people misunderstanding the meaning that I stopped telling them what it means.

The truth is we go through many births and deaths in our life. The most obvious being our physical entrance into and departure from this physical realm. But, in this modern age we've become so disconnected from our history that we've forgotten our most primal tie to the world, which is that we come from dust and return to it. We are a part of nature, after all. And while we humans perceive death as a strong word, because we fear it, most other animals in this world just perceive death for what it is—a part of life. For instance, the birth of Winter is the death of Fall. The death of adolescence is the birth of adulthood. And in this book, the death of the Initiation is the birth of the Return.

In every new phase of life, we must leave things behind. The true challenge is: how gracefully can you let go? If you listen to my past albums, you get a picture of a girl with a broken heart who's been wronged by her ex. She's sad, she's happy, she's angry, she's regretful, but more than anything, she's holding on with fists clenched. I always told myself, this was just how it had to be because I needed all this hurt to write. Yet, in moments of clarity, I'd find myself writing poems like the ones in this chapter about surrender, about missing home, and about accepting things for what they are. Some higher part of me has always wanted to be free. It has just taken a while for the rest of me to catch up.

The Hero's Journey narrative ends with a return back to the "ordinary world" with the "elixir." After departing from home to experience good and evil, I was initiated into the wisdom of the world, and now I return home with my own elixir. In this story, that elixir is surrender, or at least a sort of peaceful resignation. I don't mean not caring, or not trying, I simply mean working towards reasonable change while feeling content with the parts of myself and the world that stay constant.

These poems were written in the years 2020–2022, ages twenty-four to twenty-six. And as I finish up this book, I'm turning twenty-seven this month. I can't believe how much learning I've done this past decade. When I was twenty, I thought I was an adult, but I was so wrong. I just had the freedoms of an adult. Going out into the world with that freedom and making mistakes brought me a new lesson every year that shaped who I am now. I've had to let go of a lot of people, places, and parts of myself. And letting go was not graceful for me, it was dramatic and painful.

But now that I'm older I'm able to live life in a more peaceful way knowing that there is wisdom and meaning in every moment that comes and goes. I feel humbled by the knowledge that I can't control every experience I have. I can only control what I learn from it, and of course, what I create because of it. You might have found that there's many tales of pain and heartbreak in this book. It's not because that's all my life is, it's just where I drew a lot of inspiration from for a long time. But as you read through this last part of the book, I hope you can see how much inspiration I am drawing from the joy of just being. My past has a huge story to tell, but I'm excited to be writing the story of who I am now.

INSPIRATION

Written April 2020

Waiting on Inspiration . . .

I hear the clicks of my fan
On my low ceiling
Waiting, waiting

(Just write)

But what's the point of writing
If it's not that great?
I have a million ideas I could write down right now

But they're not good enough
To mend a heart
Or change a life

I'm looking around the room
Where is the spark?
The divine lightning strike

That flows through me and brings
Phrases that astonish
Even myself?

I am here
I am ready to bring
Forth this work

Where are you?
Will you show today?

(Just write)

But inspiration is
An amateur's good luck charm

She only dances consistently with
Those who are consistent

(Just write)

Ok, I'll write
Whether the words
Are pointless
Or nonsensical
Or brilliant

I'll write

Because inspiration is waiting for me.

INSPIRATION

Most of my songs come to me in my car, or in a crowded room, where I go to the bathroom and sing them into my phone. However, when I lived in Nashville I would often write songs for myself and others in a co-writing session. It's common for writers in Nashville to set up "co-writes" to write a song, often organized by the labels and publishers they work for. Over the last decade, co-writes with four or more people in the room have become the standard practice for producing most of the songs you hear on the radio. This is very different from the last hundred years before that, when most of the songs you heard on the radio were written by one or two people.

I felt socially pressured to co-write because it's the way people network in Nashville, but I rarely enjoyed it. I confided in one of my mentors about my disdain for this generic method of making songs and he suggested I book a weekly writer's room downtown and show up every week to write by myself. Best advice I was ever given! Alone in a room with my journal of ideas and a coffee, I wrote some of my best songs. Something about being in a room that's sole purpose is for creating was magical. Creativity's favorite command is, "Show up." When you show up enough, greatness will eventually meet you.

He's Seen Me Naked   Sept. 2017

I can't say that he
took his time
strippin me down to pride
He peeled off all my layers
but I never took off
my ~~coat~~ the first night
—CHORUS—
He's seen me naked
he's shaken hands w/my shame
He calls my demons by name
Traced the scars in
my brain, the Klaws in
my patience
now that he's done mine
& I can't look him the eye
cause he's seen me naked

I wanted ☮ so badly to
trust
This man unaffectedly
just
he handled my body
with care

He's Seen Me Naked

he's shaken hands with ~~shame~~
calls my demons by name
—fakin
—
~~Put on~~
birthmarks   —Klaws in m
                    ♡ my patience
                    —every last
                    scar in my mind

he's seen me naked
    —most vulnerable
w/his before he ever touch
eyes skin
closed   bare
                stripped
Skeletons   unguarded

    secrets

he stripped me down to
pride he @ Traced
all my Klaws w/his mind

An example of my songwriting process.
This is the original songwriting page for
"He's Seen me Naked" from my journal.
I often write phrases I want to include in
the song on the side and cross them out
as I write the lyrics.

111

SURRENDER

Written April 2020

Cotton candy skies
Purple, pink, blue, maybe a little orange
Delicate and divine
But demanding of my attention
I surrender

Pain that's so intense I clutch my chest
Regretful and wounded
New in an old way
I surrender

Voice inside of me that whispers "notice"
Soft and strong
Knower of the truth of who I am
I surrender

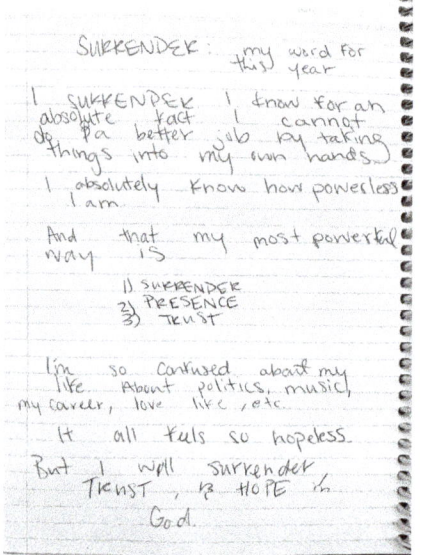

SURRENDER

Growing up, my dad used to recite Robert Service's poetry to my family all the time. I used to LOVE listening to my dad recite his poetry. Being submerged in this type of writing is what made me the poet and writer I am today, but I was never exposed to the more literary-type poetry writing. My dad always believed the best art is the kind that is the most practical and relatable. In his opinion, no one has time to interpret a bunch of pretty words.

I love his viewpoint on this, and for the most part I completely agree. That's why I write the way I write. But, I do love some interpretable pretty words. As I've evolved, I've dipped my toes into different formats of poetry and writing and have come to appreciate the art of them all.

I was explaining this once to my father, and we got into a heated discussion about rhyming vs. non-rhyming poetry. He feels strongly that poems that don't rhyme aren't poems, they're just words. I said that while I agree that some people take advantage of the format and string a bunch of nonsense together to leave "up to interpretation," there are true poets out there that do not rhyme and write incredible poetry. He disagreed, and I told him that I write some non-rhyming poems. They aren't great, but I try. Then I read him this poem, which randomly came to me while I was pumping gas and enjoying the post-sunset sky.

His reply was, "I can't call that anything but poetry."

When we all stop arguing about what art is and just take the time to listen and feel, our heart tells us what art is to us.

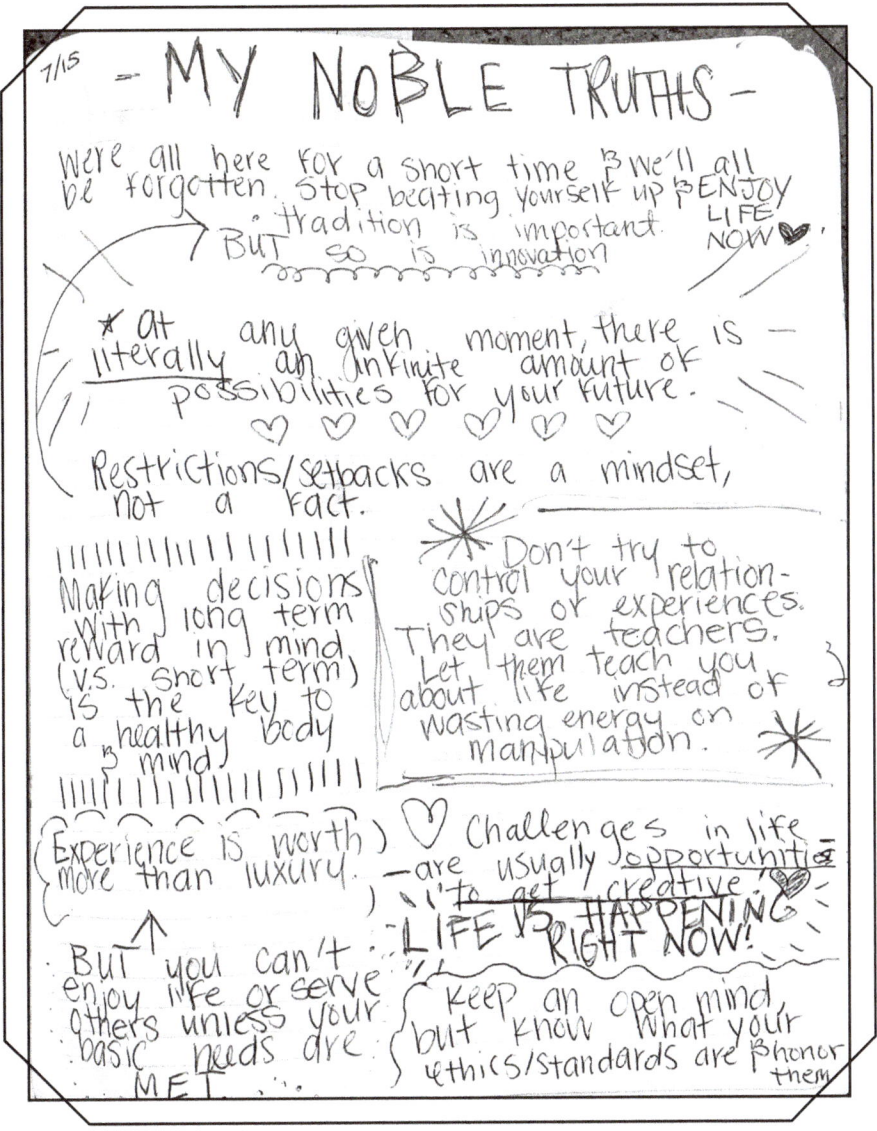

− MY NOBLE TRUTHS −

7/15

We're all here for a short time & we'll all be forgotten. Stop beating yourself up & ENJOY LIFE NOW ♥

• tradition is important. BUT so is innovation

⭐ at any given moment, there is literally an infinite amount of possibilities for your future. ♡ ♡ ♡ ♡ ♡ ♡

Restrictions/setbacks are a mindset, not a fact.

Making decisions with long term reward in mind (v.s. short term) is the key to a healthy body & mind

✳ Don't try to control your relationships or experiences. They are teachers. Let them teach you about life instead of wasting energy on manipulation. ✳

(Experience is worth more than luxury.)

♡ Challenges in life are usually opportunities to get creative ♥ LIFE IS HAPPENING RIGHT NOW!

BUT you can't enjoy life or serve others unless your basic needs are MET

Keep an open mind, but know what your ethics/standards are & honor them

A journal entry from July 2020.

113

SCARS

Written April 2020

Don't tell me of your triumphs
I know that you've come far
Don't tell me about your resume
Tell me about your scars

Don't tell me that you're here
I know right where you are
I want to know where you've been
So tell me about your scars

Every sharp edge that's cut you
And shaped you on the way
Every fall that made you think
Everything you have to say

Tell me where it hurt
And when you were without
'Cause if you were still untouched
What would we have to talk about?

And I'll show you my best self
The parts of me that are not hard
But if you really want to know me
Ask me about my scars

Freediving in mexico. Photograph taken by mike winkles.

A CONVERSATION WITH TIME

Written May 2020

Why do you always rush me?
Why do you bring me pain?
When I look forward I feel fear
When I look back I feel shame

Why do you elude me
No matter how I try?
You make hellos so fleeting
But you infinitely stretch goodbyes

Constant in your moving
The unforgiving present
Swearing not to cease
Even if I learn my lesson

You make me live my days
Afraid of running out
Mocking all the meaningless
I build my life around

Time's Response:

You act as if I've promised
To be something I'm not
But I've never promised you
A day that I will stop

I am the only constant
My rhythm, the beat of life
If I am good or bad
Has always been for you to decide

I've never claimed to heal
But they call me great at that
For only I can give the gift
Of distance from your past

If you realize I am sacred
You will see I give you mercy
Life slows down for those
Who decide they are deserving

I have never rushed you
My increments don't change
And I bet you would still curse me
If I did not stay the same

You have the same amount
As anyone, 168 hours a week
Will you continue in oblivion?
Or appreciate your mortality?

I am the grandest teacher
I show the wisdom within you
Long after you leave this earth
I will still be true

Regard me as a precious friend
Not to be cursed or killed
When you see that all you have is now
You will find I might stand still

ARBITRARY DATE

Written January 2021

Another year of cheers
To an arbitrary date
Yet still, when I wake up
I'll be the one to choose my fate

One day to reflect on
The other 364
The promises we made
We wish we'd done a little more

Who decided the starting point
Of the trip around the sun?
Who wrote the Mayan calendar?
Who made time the holy one?

This nostalgia and the lonely
When we raise our glass to cheers
Who said fresh starts only happen
One day a year

I think about these constructs
As I sit and meditate
And praise the heaven for
These 365 arbitrary dates

ARBITRARY DATE

I'm the type of person that builds things up in my head to an impossible standard and then gets really disappointed when life isn't a fairytale. When I was little, my mom and I would always stay up watching Dick Clark's NYE Show and drinking cider with some sort of cheese platter. I loved it so much. One time I fell asleep before New Year's and my mom didn't wake me up. I was so upset, the next day I made a ball out of tin foil attached to yarn and asked her to watch it drop with me!

I was in Mexico on a freediving trip a couple years ago with a friend and we went out for New Year's Eve. It was so exciting and interesting, but when midnight hit and he was FaceTiming his girlfriend, I had no one to call. It's just a lonely feeling, all that build up for nothing. I wrote this poem the next day.

BEAUTIFUL THINGS

Written January 2021

I wanted a life of Beautiful Things
As I think everyone should
So, I sought out all of the Beautiful Things
Like I promised that I would

My tires hit the highway
Every chance that I could
And I found myself inside a plane
Often, as I felt I should

I stood in front of mountains
That changed the way I think
I dove deep into the oceans
With magic underneath

I bought hand-painted treasures
To hang upon my walls
I went north in the summer
I went west in the fall

I saw rocks of such grandeur
And otherworldly trees
Canyons that moved me
And valleys that brought me to my knees

I saw so many Beautiful Things
That made me feel alive
That I couldn't understand
Why still, at night, I'd cry

Could it be because
Even in beautiful places
I could still feel pain?

Could it be that I missed,
Sitting on my porch
And listening to the rain?

Could it be that I couldn't call
These Beautiful Things
My home?

Could it be that a human being
Just isn't meant
To be alone?

So upon my arrival back
To this small place of mine
I noticed some beautiful things
I'd been missing all this time

The way my nieces sprint
To embrace me with a hug
The way my father sings
The way my mother loves

How everyone at the local shop
For coffee knows my name
The way we sit upon the porch
And listen to the rain

I still dream about the big trees
That forever changed my mind
And I know I will return
Back to the mountains when it's time

And I believe that you must leave
And learn things on your own to grow
But I think that the most Beautiful Things
Are to love and be loved, to know and be known.

BEAUTIFUL THINGS

I traveled and toured so much in my early twenties and I thought I'd never get tired of it. Until one day, I just did. I wanted to be home with the people I love. I grew up in a small town and I always made fun of the people who never left. But now, I sort of get it. I'll never regret the four years I spent living in Nashville and everything I learned there. It's important to leave, to go and open up your mind. But I realized that the most vital thing to me is family. This is why I spend this season of my life near my family!

OFTEN

Written January 2021

Often I fantasize,
That I die
And you realize how much you loved me all along
Then you finally regret
All the times
You could've kissed me,
but didn't

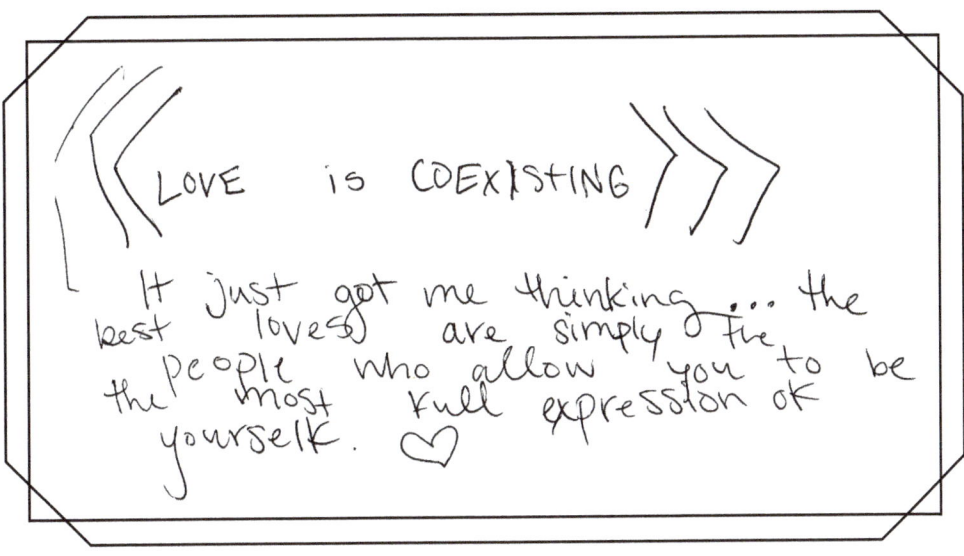

« LOVE is COEXISTING »»

It just got me thinking ... the
best loves are simply the
the people who allow you to be
most full expression of
yourself. ♡

A journal entry from 2021.

WANDERESS

Written February 2021

Nothing's stranger than being a stranger everywhere that you go
But I've never known something ever, better to make me grow
Sometimes I cry at night when I look up at the stars
'Cause I've never felt more content, but there's still an emptiness in my heart
So I roll on, and I stop at a little town
Run into a woman who offers to show me around
Well

Do you know a place where I can fill up?
Tell me about your husband, are you in love?
Hey, where is the diner where all of the waitresses
Call you by name?
Do you got a way we could stay in touch?
Hope we meet again and thanks for the lunch
I just have one last unusual question, I must confess
Do you know a wanderer who's lookin' for a wanderess?

I drove through the desert, never imagined a heat like that
Made friends on the way who told me their secrets and I told mine back
I've hiked through the Badlands, pitched tents in the dark and been brought to my knees
But what good is a memory with no one to share it with but me
So I roll on, I don't mind driving through the night
Might stop for a cigar and when somebody asks for a light,
I'll say

Do you know a place where I can fill up?
Married 40 years, wow, that must be love
Hey, where is the diner where all of the waitresses
Call you by name?
Do you got a way we could stay in touch?
Hope we meet again and thank you so much
I just have one last unusual question, I must confess
Do you know a wanderer who's lookin' for a wanderess?

I'm not saying that I'd change it if I can
What I've been through is what made me who I am
There's so many things I only noticed cause I was alone
I don't wanna stop wondering, just wanna call another wanderer home
So

I'm gonna grab a coffee and top off the tank
In a couple hours somewhere on the way
I'll stop at a diner where all of the waitresses call me by name
I'll probably set up camp by the river tonight
Probably talk to God while I'm building the fire
And until we meet again, just know that I'm safe and content
But let me know
If you meet a wanderer who's lookin' for a wanderess

do you know a
Wanderer who's lookin
for a
Wanderess?

Today's meditation's intention:
BEING

Being is...
presence, paying attention to the good & bad
feels inside your body & mind.
Being gentle w/them, connecting w/
them, giving time to them.

relinquishing control,

surrendering

God is... seeing the gratitude
on the waiter's face
this morning when we
gave him a big tip.

Trying to communicate w/
someone who speaks a
different language than you,
the give & take, the universal
language.

CREATE (A MAKER'S PSALM)

Written March 2021

Babies are born
People are buried
The sun rises and sets
And I will create

Couples separate
Couples are married
Gamblers win and lose bets
And I will create

The soft pulse of life
Tragic and joyful
Beats in a language
I'll try to translate

Into a prose
That capture's a story
Of universal truth
That's what I'll make

Mountains stand tall
And grander than I
Could ever imagine
And for whose sake?

The ocean has depths
That no living human
Can ever descend to
And why is it that way?

Someone is crying
And someone is loving
It seems that life's theme
Is grieve then celebrate

So, someone must try
To remember these quarries
Before we are dust
And so, I will Make

Yes, someone must say
What someone else can't
Express on their own
And so, I Create

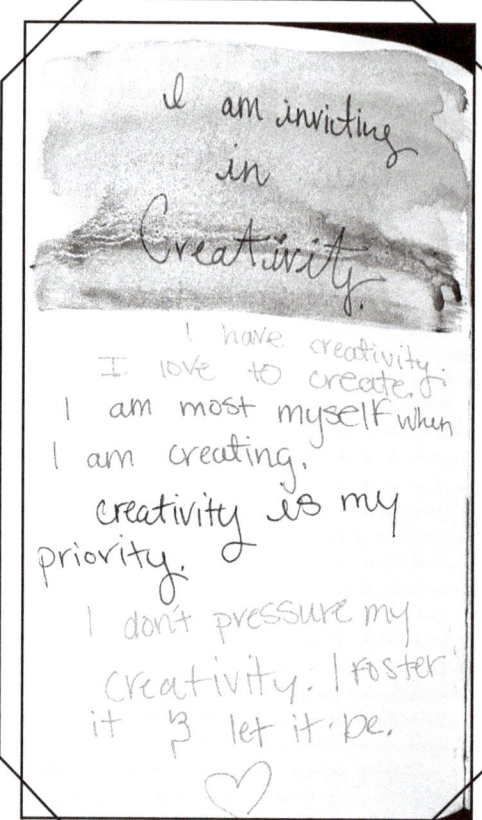

I am inviting
in
Creativity.

I have creativity.
I love to create.
I am most myself when
I am creating.
creativity is my
priority.
I don't pressure my
creativity. I foster
it & let it be.
♡

A journal entry on creativity written in 2021.

Good morning.

It is so chilly today so I am cozily sitting outside writing. I woke up feeling depressed but writing helped restore me.

Creating is what I am leaning into because it is how I get closest to God. God is a divine creator & when I create I am connected to him through his most sacred act.

Therefore, I am committing to starting my mornings w/ a free write & journaling. The first routine that seems very important to me. →

COLORS

Written May 2021

I was the colors
To your grayscale world
I gave you an oyster
You took out the pearl

You sketched up a design
That you couldn't shade
I added striking hues
Of magnificent paint

I made you notice
The wind on your face
I asked you to dance
In every empty space

When you spun me around
Did you forget to care?
About who you hurt?
About who else was there?

And now that I'm gone
Taking with me my bright
Will you smile in your world
Of just black and white?

SHAKING

Written May 2021

Oh my God, it's been a year
Since you stood in front of me
But now you're standing right here
I used to dream about when this day would come
And I remember the day I stopped caring if it ever would
I avoid the places you go
And the days you go there casually
But I don't keep a calendar
So I knew that I'd slip up eventually

I don't ever want you back
I wouldn't wish what we had
On anybody else
So why is my body shutting down?
The memories that I forgot
Come in butterflies and knots
But I don't want you anymore
So what am I shaking for?

You don't measure up to the man of my memory
He stood much taller
And he had the nerve to say hello to me
Well thank you for the confirmation of the bullet I dodged
But something about being so close to you has me missing that scar
'Cause I see you in that T-shirt
And I feel nostalgic for those memories
I'm a stronger woman now
And I don't like how you still make me weak

I don't ever want you back
I wouldn't wish what we had
On anybody else
So why is my body shutting down?
The memories that I forgot
Come in butterflies and knots
But I don't want you anymore
So what am I shaking for?

SHAKING

I wrote this song after running into someone I used to date at a show. I had been over him for a long time, but something about seeing him brought up all the memories and I found my hands shaking as I walked away from the interaction. I literally drove home and asked myself, "Megan, you don't want him anymore, so what are you shaking for?" And then I thought, "Well, that rhymes so . . ." I sang the chorus into my phone on the way home and finished the song later that night.

SUN SETTLING

Written August 2021

Interesting that we say the sun sets
When it doesn't move at all
We do.

To say the sun sets
Almost implies that it settles
But why would we expect the brightest star within our reach to settle?

We're the ones who settle
We settle in for a night's sleep
Sometimes we settle for things less comfortable than that . . .

I am on a plane rushing through the sky
And I see the colors of the sunset all around me as I head west
But I don't know where to look. Where is my focal point?

The closer I get to the sun the further away it gets from setting
We could continue this dance forever
Well, no. The sun could. I could not.

Eventually I will get tired and need rest
Eventually my body will get tired and rest forever
The sun doesn't set. I do.

But I need not think about all that today
As I blast through the sky on a moving machine defying gravity
In the high noon of my youth, long before the sunset of my life
Enjoying the pastels of the sky from a sun that never sets.

SUN SETTLING

A couple years ago I went on a solo trip to Hawaii to stay with some friends. I was trying to get over a heartbreak that was particularly hard for me because of how many adventures we had shared together, so I wanted to have a new adventure of my own. Nearing the end of a 24-hour travel day, I was on my last flight, from California to Hawaii, and I was feeling so over it. The 5-hour flight to Big Island was one with no Wi-Fi, so I just sat there looking out the window at the sky. It was so strange to see the sun in that moment. It was setting, but we were outrunning the actual "set" and it just looked like this eternal light stuck in the sky. It was a sunset that never set. This view totally inspired me, and I found myself writing this piece.

WHAT IF

Written September 2021

What if, what if, what if
It drives my mind all day long

What if, what if, what if
Like a bird it is my song

What if that never happened?
What if they never left?

I entertain so many almosts
I may what if myself to death

What if I never said it
What if I knew what I know now

Would things be so much better?
Would they still be around?

But wait, if he had stayed
Would I have this perspective?

Would I have learned the things I've learned
Without the imperfections?

And what about this life?
I've lived it to the fullest

Would I have learned to live
If I had truly been less foolish?

What if, what if, what if,
My wishes, my regrets

But if I had a time machine
Would I just make a different mess?

The ratio of pain to joy
Would it be so vastly changed?

Or would I just feel happiness
And hurt in different ways?

What if, what if, what if,
My anchor to the past

What if I'm who I am
Only because of what I've lost and had?

P.S.
And what if this moment
Is all I'll ever really have?

Freediving in Mexico.
Photograph taken
by Mike Winkles.

FREE

Written October 2021

It has come to my attention
That I think I'm finally free
Because I want to be with him
And I still want to be me

It has been brought to my awareness
That I must've finally changed
Because I want to have a big love
But I still want to have my space

I think that I can finally call myself my
inspiration
Because for the first time
In my life
My needs aren't out of desperation

I must be ruled by wisdom
Instead of things I feel
Because I finally know the worth
Of something that's rooted and real

The voice of fear's gone quiet
And the voice of doubt has moved on
Sovereign is inner me
Who wants the will of God

My pride is understanding
And my heart still beats unhindered
I never dreamed that it would be
This easy to surrender

It has come to my attention
That I think I'm finally free
Because I live and love
Like the woman I always prayed to be

FREE

In my late teens and early twenties, I used to overreact when things went wrong in ways that were desperate and childish. No matter what I tried I couldn't stop myself in the moment. I lived for so long with this fear that I would never find a love that lasted because there is something wrong with me that scares people off. As you've read, I learned over the years that I simply needed to heal some past experiences that were affecting my present. Being in therapy helped me take responsibility for my emotions in a healthy way and stop being a victim. The cognitive therapy methods that helped me immensely are IFS and EMDR.

I wrote this poem about my first happy, stable relationship after this healing experience. I'm not perfect, but I'm able to take ownership of my own life and live in a way I'm proud of now. I no longer live with the belief that I'm unlovable. What I never thought could happen, has happened, thanks to my hard inner-work, my incredible therapist, and the support system around me. I'm finally free.

FOLLOW ME

Written November 2021

A year and a few months ago I ran into a boy
He told me that he wanted to make me his pride and joy
And that's when I began to hear this voice inside my head
This irresponsible advisor talking from my chest

Follow me, don't you wanna feel that rush
Follow me, I'm the one that you should trust
Follow me, and worst case you'll get a song
Follow me, what could possibly go wrong

Well that one didn't work out, oh but who am I to blame
I can't predict the future, but I can decide your fate
And look at this one's eyes, those are eyes that don't betray
Trust me girl, you'll be thanking me when it comes your wedding day

Follow me, don't you wanna feel that rush
Follow me, I'm the one that you should trust
Follow me, and worst case you'll get a song
Follow me, what could possibly go wrong

At least you can say you took the chance, you didn't run
And at your life's end you'll understand you were brave enough to love

Follow me, don't you wanna feel that rush
Follow me, I'm the one that you should trust
Follow me, and worst case you'll get a song
Follow me, what could possibly go wrong

FOLLOW ME

I was getting ready for a date and beforehand I'd been going through some of my old journals. I found this little doodle I made of a heart with a bruise and Band-Aid on it saying "Follow Me" in my journal. I thought it was really telling of my experience with love and I immediately started singing the lyrics into my phone as I was getting ready. I wrote this song in twenty minutes, just singing it into my phone and later put it down in writing to my guitar. It's definitely one of those writing experiences where it felt like a stream of consciousness coming through me. Creating is not usually like that, but we show up and keep writing so that we may experience those divine moments.

The doodle I found in my journal that inspired "Follow me."

ODE TO THE CRANE

Written December 2021

I ride my bike across this path at least once a day,
To say hello to the neighborhood and exercise my legs,
Across the sleepy road, past the schoolyard, to the lake,
I turn the wheels of this contraption till dark creeps my way,

But you'd be surprised to know my favorite part of the route,
It's a corner lot with a quiet home not too far from my house,
There in the yard is a bird, its left leg nowhere to be found,
I pass her every day as she hobbles all around,

I do not know exactly when this sweet, sad crane appeared,
How she lost her leg or why she chose to reside here,
If she's been around a decade or if this is her first year,
Or why she never chooses to resign to all her fears,

What particularly saddens me is this fact I've known a while,
That cranes are monogamous creatures that only have one mate for life,
And my mind begins to wonder whatever was this bird's past strife,
Did she lose her lover and her leg all at the same time?

But all that I can do is ride beside her once a day,
As she hops along in search of bugs or rests beneath the shade,
I can't reach out and pet her she'd attack or be afraid,
And so, I just say a quiet prayer that she's content and safe,

I hope that she is young and merely born with this dysfunction,
That someday she'll have a family that hobbles with her in conjunction,
Why was she given this fate? I ask God each day in compunction,
But she doesn't seem to mind as she fulfills her day's consumption,

So, I send love and grace as I pass her silhouette,
I wonder if she feels it or just sees me as a threat,
I wish that I could tell her she's my personal vignette,
Of the courage of a crane with one leg I'll never forget.

ODE TO THE CRANE

This is one of my favorite poems I've written recently. When I'm in Florida with my parents, my mom and I go for bike rides around town in the evening. I grew up in a one-stoplight town, so you can pretty much cover the area in an hour bike ride. In the small town of Geneva, Florida, that I hail from, sandhill cranes run absolutely rampant. They are all over the place! You have to dodge them in the road when riding a bike, and as beautiful as they are, they are mean! I'm pretty terrified of them!

But, this particular week, as I went on my bike rides alone, I kept passing this small crane, usually resting in the grass, or grazing on one leg. Because of the way cranes stand, it took me a while to realize she was missing the bottom half one of her legs. Something about this made me so sad, and I had all of these questions for her. After pondering for a few days as I passed her, I came home from a bike ride one day and immediately wrote this one in my journal.

COLORS

Written December 2021

Aces in hand and your name on my plans
We cashed in the chips before we finished our hand
Always on the run, secrets are fun
That's what you told me as you loaded the gun

Would've done anything for you
You knew me inside out
I rolled the dice 'cause I loved you
A fixed game always goes to the house

Vulnerable, my soul bare before you
I turned my cheek to the gray lines that you drew
Never will I give love to another
I showed my cards, you showed your colors

Beautiful hues that I thought made you you
Were only reflecting off a light that was mine
Words that you said, I wrote them in red
I made my bets thinking you were on my side

You were my strength and my weakness
I trusted you to Mars
Gave you my sacred oath but
You crossed your fingers when you crossed your heart

Vulnerable, my soul bare before you
I turned my cheek to the gray lines that you drew
Never will I give love to another
I showed my cards, you showed your colors

Yeah

I saw your heart and your heart was black
Tilted the tables standing behind my back
Took the money and ran
That's what I get for showing my hand

Vulnerable, my soul bare before you
I turned my cheek to the gray lines that you drew
Never will I give love to another
I showed my cards, you showed your colors

I DON'T WRITE LOVE SONGS

Written February 2022

No, I don't write love songs
I have no reason to
I don't follow Cupid's arrow
I follow the arrow of truth

It's not that I don't believe in love
It's obvious I'm its disciple
It's just that love has yet to give me
Anything but a vicious cycle

Yes, I don't write love songs
Because I'm not in love
And even when I fall in love
It's not something worthy of

A melody that's dedicated
To a partner pure and honest
Toxicity doesn't inspire
Shakespearean love sonnets

And I'm very sad to say
Toxicity is all I've known
The passion, anger, chaos
I'm drawn to it like a home

But I know it's not the place
I want to call my home forever
To start to learn of real love
Now, there is no time that's better

So no, I don't write love songs
And it's not because I refuse
I'd be delighted to pen a serenade
With desire and adoring infused

I don't write love songs, so far
Because it hasn't been my time
But when my heart finds a healthy home
I'm sure I'll hear a rhyme

WALLFLOWER

Written March 2022

Once I was only a wallflower
Watching the bees in the room
I laughed when they laughed
And answered when they asked
And only on their account did I move

Once I was only a seedling
Hundreds of days from a bloom
I watched everyone else
Stand taller than myself
While others admired their fruit

Once I was just a young daisy
With pedals of my very own yellow
I dreamed to be pretty
I hoped that they'd pick me
But they found my color too mellow

Once I became a sunflower
Bright and beautiful, sun on my face
It'd been long since the day
I grew slow in the shade
Too afraid to take up my own space

And as I grew taller and stronger
Others came from afar for my nectar
Sweet and potent it was
From all of the love and wisdom
That I had collected

I remembered, once I was a wallflower
An observer so small in the room
It wasn't time for my turn
And I'm glad that I learned
the beauty in a belated bloom

THE GAME

Written May 2022

I was the worst waitress that the Fish Camp's ever seen
I remember being teased for taking time off to chase my dream
I'd have nightmares I'd forget to bring ranch to the table in the restaurant yard
And when my small town friends screwed me over again I'd always take it hard
Yeah I'd look in the mirror
And I'd cry as I'd pray
I came here to tell the truth
Not play the game

Four years in a ten-year town and that was enough for me
Sacrifice ain't the same as selling your soul to a so-called dream
I knew how to work hard, I was raised that way, never had no problem with that
Daddy raised a girl with sweat on her brow, didn't raise me to kiss no ass
But I had to do that
If I wanted to stay
People asked what was wrong
I remember I'd say
I came here to tell the truth
Not play the game

Honesty ain't for everyone but it's all there was for me
They'd tell me to be original then curse my originality
Sittin' with four guys in a room to write a three-minute song
How many people does it take to tell the truth and still end up getting it wrong
But I tried to belong
Took my heart out the song
At the end of the day
Oh, Nashville, you've changed
And I came here to tell the truth
Not play the game

Here I am back home again

Yeah I hear how the people talk

But I never wanted to make it to the big stage

By being someone I'm not

But I still feel the possibility

When my hands curl around this guitar

How can they say I haven't made it

When my God we've come this far

And it's still just the start

Map drawn on my heart

In it for the long haul

Not five minutes of fame

When I think of why I'm on this Earth

And why I am this way—

I came here to tell the truth

Not play the game

THE GAME

In past chapters, you've read my stories about struggling with the music industry and why I left Nashville. Like most artists, COVID-19 set my career back extensively. The majority of my income comes from home concerts and live shows. I tried to suffice with online, but ultimately it led to a huge loss of income that left me scrambling the past few years. It has taken courage to finally start planning the release of new projects in such uncharted territory.

Additionally, staying back in Florida where I was raised has been a wonderful and strange experience for me. On one hand, I feel very connected to my past and my creative spark. On the other hand, it's very uncomfortable to run into old acquaintances and explain why I've moved back for the time being. People judge. They laugh. They get pity in their eyes and say things like, "What a shame you didn't make it in Nashville."

I feel mournful and embarrassed. But what I can't explain to most people in such a short amount of time is that I didn't give up. I chose to follow my own path. To "make it" in my own way by building on a relationship with my fans and not playing the game. I chose longevity and personal happiness over a soulless pursuit to fame.

I hope I win a Grammy one day. I hope that you will "see me on TV" as so many people told me they would when I was a kid. But, after dealing with the pressure of trying to be a star and make everyone proud for two-thirds of my life, I just couldn't anymore. If I "make it" it will be by putting out authentic art like this book you have in your hands. It will be by hugging my fans and laughing and crying with them. It will be by pouring my heart out, and not kissing anyone's ass.

And for the record, when I write this book for you, when I sing my songs to you, when I travel the country to connect with you, I feel sure in my heart that I've already made it.

DRAMA QUEEN

Written June 2022

I used to be a drama queen,
Keeping careful count,
Of everyone who hurt me, pushed me down, or pushed me out.

I used to be a victim,
A constant cry for help,
I'd spend my days wishing for the pity of someone else.

"How dare they," I would cry,
"Not feel what I'm going through!"
I wish someone would've told me it's no one's to feel but you.

The things that happened to me,
Happened for me, happened by me,
I'd relinquish my responsibility and make myself so tiny.

I used to be a drama queen,
Till one day I got bored,
Of making other people the thing that I live for.

I used to be a drama queen,
Sharing with the world my strife,
Until I dipped my toes in taking ownership of my life.

And while I started taking care
Of this life in my name,
I realized that composure is more powerful than blame.

And though everything in my body
Screamed to fight, and yell, and hate,
I finally found the power in simply walking away.

I made my circle smaller
And tried this thing called boundaries,
And for the first time in my life I became addicted to peace.

And when I am done wrong,

And others expect me to fight them,

I realized what truly drives them crazy is my silence.

So, I used to be a drama queen,

I don't blame my sweet past self,

I know all she truly wanted was to be understood by someone else.

Yeah, I used to be a drama queen,

But that's no longer me,

'Cause I decided not to let the world tell me who I'll be.

DRAMA QUEEN

Anyone who's known me a while can tell you that in the past few years I've become a much more mellow person. I've drawn boundaries and built up a dignity I never thought I could possess. It's taken a lot of experience, tears, and therapy, but these days I value my privacy and dignity much more than I value my drama.

I have a friend who is a bit younger than me, and she used to call me every few days to tell me a new story about someone who hurt her. Her life was so full of drama, and she was so sincerely invested. I supported her and loved her, but I had to chuckle a bit, because she reminded me of my younger self. Thinking about that inspired this poem. You think everything is a big deal when you're young but then you grow up and realize you were quite silly. And that is totally okay in my book. (Literally.)

I DON'T KNOW WHAT LOVE IS

Written July 2022

I don't know what love is
I don't know what it means
Every time that I have it
I think it's magic
Until it's mean

Does it start with a kiss
Does it start with a word
Does it start with an action
Or a contract, or a verb?

Is it wild sex with your crazy ex?
'Cause I got that down pat
Is it diamond rings and shiny things?
'Cause I've also done that
Is it obsession? Or depression?
Had it both ways and I must say

I don't know what love is
I don't know how to stay
I don't know how to leave
I was fine blaming everyone else
But myself
When I was 23

But now I'm 26 and I want a kid
And I want a picket fence
And I start to make an argument
But realize it don't make sense
My pride is great but it can't
Keep me warm in bed
I said that I don't know what love is

But I know I want it
And I need it
For so long now I've been dreaming

He will be mine and
I will be his
Soon as I can figure out what love is

Do you know what love is?
Have you had it before?
Cause I heard 50 percent of marriages
Wind up in divorce

That's a depressing statistic
But you get what I'm sayin'
Don't wanna end up an addict
Or a number
Or a cliche

'Cause I've been all of those things
But now the thrill is getting old
And it makes for a great song
But it don't make for a great home
I'll grow up now
Figure it out
'Cause I'll probably never ever know what love is

But I know I want it
And I need it
For so long now I've been dreaming
He will be mine and
I will be his
Soon as I can figure out what love is

I don't know what love is

I DON'T KNOW WHAT LOVE IS

A few months ago, I was lying awake in bed. It was extremely early in the morning and I couldn't go back to sleep. I struggle with insomnia, and when I have moments that I can't sleep, my brain starts doing this really weird thing where it asks me repetitive questions in my head that I don't know the answers to. This morning, the obsession was, "What is love?" I kid you not, I laid there awake for over an hour trying to figure out what the hell love is and what it means. Finally, when I knew I wasn't going back to sleep, I got up and walked to my keyboard and wrote this in ten minutes. It was just a contemplation that ended up being sort of catchy. Please do let me know if you know what love is.

I am anointed with courage.

I AM HERE TO LEARN TO TRUST.

I am rooted in Gratitude.

I
ASK
HARD
QUESTIONS
&

relax
into the
mystery.

I am here
to
TEACH
honesty.

I am

Perception

A journal entry from 2021.

RETURN

My friend, it's been a journey

And though I've crashed and burned

Oh, how blessed

I am to rest

And digest what I've learned

I've catastrophized and analyzed

Round every twist and turn

But, oh, how kind

Proclaims my mind

Life's been to me, unearned

I'm but a mile now from town

And now that my trip adjourns

Oh, how sweet,

My tired feet feel

Now that I've returned

Photograph taken
by Emily Richo.

EPILOGUE

I grew up on stories. I come from a small town where every old guy who came into the Fish Camp where I worked had something clever to say. While most people brushed them off, I listened intently and delighted at the punchline or moral to every tale, every joke, every lesson. I've always found that I get along better with my elders than my peers, and I suspect this is because they have so much to share. While I don't have the richness and wisdom of a life full of stories that they do, I do have my truth, and that's what I've tried to share with you in this book.

Being born in '96, I'm one of the last generations who grew up with VCRs, landlines, and tinker toys. I watched the world around me change as kids acquired iPhones in my high school years and I have despaired as the world has become increasingly disconnected with our own humanity. My friends often tease me and call me old fashioned, a ninety-year-old living in a twenty-something's body. But is it old fashioned to miss speaking with your neighbor? Is it old fashioned to prefer the whispers of the trees over the hum of a computer? Or is it simply human nature? What's the common thread that connects us all and why do we feel more disconnected than ever?

As an artist, I've been given a unique opportunity to observe others from an outside perspective and I believe that it's taught me a lot about truth. The truth is our stories are what makes us great. This is our ancestral bond, the pathway to empathy and relating to the world around us, and we've been missing it. However, I have hope in knowing that we aren't missing it because it's not there, but rather it's not what's highlighted in our culture. In a culture that glorifies the picture perfect, we often don't get to hear about the ache that brought others to where they are. The messiness. Their own hero's journey.

I was raised in the world of the simple and the downhome. There's so much to love about that life and the people that live it. Interestingly enough, while most people don't consider us country folk artistic, we do love our stories. We love to sing songs by the fire, we love to make each other laugh, and ultimately stories are how we relate to and learn from each other. It's always been my favorite thing about the culture.

However, I never completely fit in where I was raised. I was always drawn to the hippies, the explorers, and the eccentric. Going out on tour to other cities and places, I was given the opportunity to insert myself into the unfamiliar lives of others and experience the contrast between my life and theirs. But I was amazed at how much we had in common. I fell in love with the people I met all over the country because I realized we speak the same language—story.

Being a country girl and a hippie all at once, I often feel I have my feet in two worlds. I love this, because I get to love more people and things about life through an open mind. My mind is open because I listened. I took so much pleasure in listening to the stories of others and telling them my own. A story is a pathway from one human to another, no matter how different they may be. When you tell your story, another sees their own inside it and you are united through your laughter or tears.

I hope this book might give you the courage to tell your own stories. Because you never know who's listening. But more importantly, you never know who needs to hear it.

THANK YOU

Written September 2018

I woke up this morning
Filled up my lungs
Sweet, fresh air
That never runs out
Thank you.

I smiled at a stranger
Their eyes looking into mine
The funny experience of life
We share in common
Thank you.

I ordered my favorite coffee
Dark, flavorful aroma
Happy stream oozing from the top
I sip it slow
Thank you.

I felt contentedness
Pain, joy, anger, bliss
All in one day
Tomorrow I get to do it again
Thank you.

ACKNOWLEDGMENTS

With deep and eternal gratitude, I'd like to give thanks and praise to those who've supported me in making this long-time dream a reality.

First and foremost, my gratitude is to God for giving me the gift of artistic perception and articulation. I know this is not something I can take credit for because my writing often comes through me and not from me. But most of all, I know this gift is not my own by how it touches others in ways I never thought I could with my own human words. I'm in humble awe of this honor. All the glory and thanks to God!

To the incredible supporters of my work who've stuck by my side and always encouraged me to be myself, this includes everyone who has hosted me for a house concert, been a Patreon patron, an incredible fan, or all of the above, I thank you immensely. I'd like to specifically mention some of my fans who've become family to me, including Gina and Kenny Ergun, Jen Singer, Billy Michels, Sheri and Hugh Hoeger, Amanda Olaffson, Kate Halkett, Garrett Ellenz, Mike Little, Diane and Jeff Davitt, and so many more. Each of you have changed my life and perspective at some point by our conversations. You've welcomed me into your life, a fellow artist and misfit, and you've loyally supported my artistic ventures from our first meeting. I wish I could explain how much this means to me. I love you all so deeply and I am forever grateful for you.

Speaking of fans who've became dear friends, I have to thank Steve and Azul as well as the entire team at Authors Who Lead. Steve and Azul, from the moment I met you I felt I had found my people. You inspire me just by being yourselves. Thank you for believing in me as an artist and giving my message a platform. You two have helped me to dream big and enjoy the details of life. I love you so much. And to the team at Authors Who Lead, you transformed my book into something I'm extremely proud of. This venture is only possible because of the heart, clarity, and support you provided. THANK YOU!!!

My utmost gratitude and thanks to my wonderful friends and photographers that took a few of the photos in this book: Mike Winkles, whose photography can be found at @narcosis27 on Instagram. And Emily Richo of Submerged Dreams Photography, whose photography can be found at @submergeddreams on Instagram. I admire your artistry and mutual love and advocacy for the springs and this amazing state of ours. Thanks for creating art with me!

Thank you to my mom and dad who used to stay up late listening to me play my songs in the living room, who believed in me when it would've been easier to tell me to choose a different career, and who've been my best friends, biggest fans, and greatest supporters since I was a kid singing Martina McBride at the talent show. I don't take lightly the sacrifices you've made to support me, and I want you to know how much I love you and look up to you. I strive to always make you proud.

Lastly, I owe a huge amount of gratitude to you, the reader, for holding this book in your hand and reading my story. Your support means everything to me, and I write for you always. Thank you!

I am
Grateful
for
this
Moment

ABOUT MEGAN

Megan Katarina is an award-winning singer-songwriter and poet. She inspires audiences to connect to themselves and each other through her relatable and vulnerable storytelling and interactive performances. Since the age of thirteen, Megan has been touring and playing all over Florida and the US. In summer of 2017, she moved to Nashville. In April of 2018, she released her first full-length album, *Being Crazy Ain't for the Weak*, produced by Jared Anderson and recorded live at OmniSound Studios. The album went #14 on iTunes and was received and loved on a global scale.

In February of 2020, just after returning home from a long year of multiple house concert tours across the US, she released her new album, *To Be Honest*, an acoustic album in tribute to the intimate storytelling setting of her house concerts, in which a beautiful connection between artist and listener is forged.

Megan not only writes for herself but for many other rising artists. She has charted with multiple artists on iTunes like Tana Matz, Ryan Robinette, and Tyler Rich. Her own song "He's Seen Me Naked" placed third out of 2,500+ submissions in the 2017 NSAI songwriting competition.

Megan's writing shines in the honest way she portrays the ironic, heartbreaking, funny, and less attractive sides of life through her quirky humor and sincere voice, inspiring resilience with her words. Her relatability is what makes her relationship with her fans so strong, as if they are more like long-lost friends. Respected for doing things her own way, Megan continues to rise and gain recognition through a loyal social media following and live shows alike.

Remember to check out the SECRET ALBUM at

www.megankatarina.com/storiedalbum

To follow more of my music and poetry, visit me at

www.megankatarina.com

And if you enjoyed this book,
please leave a REVIEW on Amazon.

www.ingramcontent.com/pod-product-compliance
Lightning Source LLC
Chambersburg PA
CBHW041535120626
46551CB00019B/2709

* 9 7 9 8 9 8 8 6 3 8 6 0 5 *